Homesteading for Beginners

*A Budget-Friendly Path To
A Self-Sufficient Lifestyle*

Elise Baker

The Green Homesteader

Copyright © 2022 Elise Baker

ISBN: 978-1-959372-00-4 Paperback

ISBN: 978-1-959372-01-1 Hardcover

All rights reserved, including the right to reproduce this book or portions thereof in any form whatsoever.

No part of this publication may be reproduced, distributed, stored in a retrieval system or transmitted in any form or by any means, including photocopying, recording, or other electronic or mechanical methods, without the prior written permission of the publisher, except in the case of brief quotations embodied in critical reviews and certain other noncommercial uses permitted by copyright law. For permission requests, write to the publisher, addressed "Attention: Permissions Coordinator," at the address above.

Cover by Vindysign
Illustrated by Alina Levandovska

Published by The Green Homesteader
PO Box 6164
Sparta, TN 38583
https://www.TheGreenHomesteader.com

Acknowledgements

Publishing a book has been more work than I ever anticipated, and I could not have accomplished this work without the support of my Facebook friends who reviewed the advance release and provided helpful feedback.

And of special mention is my son's friend Megan. She spent considerable time proof reading and editing. Her comments were insightful and helped define the overall tone of the book.

I'd also like to thank my illustrator, Alina. She was able to take concepts and photos and turn them into the beautiful silhouettes you see throughout this book.

Of course, I can't forget my awesome AIA Mastermind groups and accountability partner, Eve, who helped me get over some of the disheartening hurdles that were found along the way to becoming published.

And finally, I'd like to thank the Mikkelsen twins without whose education and support none of this would have been possible. They provided the encouragement and resources necessary to make publishing a reality.

CONTENTS

PART 1: HOMESTEADING ESSENTIALS 1

CHAPTER 1: WHAT IS HOMESTEADING? 2
- Why Do People Homestead? 3
- Three Essential Homesteading Terms and Their Context 4
- Homesteading in the Modern World 5

CHAPTER 2: HOMESTEADERS, PREPPERS, AND SURVIVALISTS 8
- What is a Prepper? 9
- What is a Survivalist? 10
- Preppers and Survivalists and Homesteaders, Oh My 11

CHAPTER 3: EVERYONE HAS DIFFERENT MOTIVATIONS 16
- Lifestyle Choices Offer More Freedom 17
- Food Storage is a Defining Factor 18
- Caring For Medicinal Needs 18
- Water Options for Homesteaders, Preppers, and Survivalists 19
- Life Off-the-Grid 20
- Security of a Homestead 21
- Homesteaders Are a Breed of Our Own 22

CHAPTER 4: THE HOMESTEADING LIFESTYLE 24
- It's a Wonderful Life – The Many Benefits of Homesteading 25

CHAPTER 5: THINGS I WISH I HAD KNOWN BEFORE I STARTED 32
- The Reality of Off-The-Grid Living 33
- The Three Biggest Setbacks of Homesteading 36
- Other Common Homesteading Mistakes 38

PART 2: FINDING YOUR REASON 41

CHAPTER 6: IS HOMESTEADING FOR ME? 42
- Analysis Paralysis 45
- Reason #1: Declare Financial Freedom 45

- Reason #2: Provide your Own Food 48
- Reason #3: Lead a Healthier Lifestyle 49
- Reason #4: Going Green 52

FREE GOODWILL 56

CHAPTER 7: CAN I MAKE MONEY FROM HOMESTEADING? 58
- Monetizing Your Homestead Requires a Touch of Creativity 59

CHAPTER 8: WHAT DOES IT COST TO GET STARTED? 66
- Know Your Family's Needs 66
- Costs Associated with Homesteading 67
- Starting a Homestead with Little to No Money 69
- Create a Budget Right Now! 69
- Prepare for Tax Laws Associated with Homesteading 70
- Homestead Exemption 73
- Local Agricultural Tax Breaks 74
- Local Farming Programs 75
- Grant Opportunities 75
- Veterans Benefits 75

PART 3: MAKE SURE YOU'RE COMMITTED 77

CHAPTER 9: THE BEGINNER'S GARDEN 78
- Starting a Small Garden 79
- Easiest Vegetables to Grow 83
- Five Easy Herbs for Beginners to Grow 91
- Medicinal Herbs 93

CHAPTER 10: PICKLING AND CANNING 96
- What Produce Can be Pickled? 97
- Pickling Tips 98
- Canning For Beginners 99
- Water Bath Canning Versus Pressure Canning 99

PART 4: START A SUCCESSFUL HOMESTEAD 103

CHAPTER 11: PROVIDING FOR YOUR FAMILY 104
Calculating Your Family's Needs 105

CHAPTER 12: SET YOUR FINALIZED GOALS 112
Year One Expectations 113
Gardening 114
Determine What Structures You Need to Build 118
Creating a Layout of Your Homestead 120

CHAPTER 13: CREATE A PLAN OF EXECUTION 124
Identify Tasks and Make a To-Do List 126
Weekly Planning Made Simple 127

FINAL THOUGHTS 130
ABOUT THE AUTHOR 131
YOUR OPINION MATTERS! 132
REFERENCES 133

Bonus Content

As a thank you for purchasing this book you will have access to Free Bonus Content. As we continue to publish new books and content this will get updated.

Currently we are offering the following supporting content:

- Budget Planner and Smart Goal Setting Workbook – Start planning and managing your homestead expenses with this free download.
- Planting Calculator – Quickly figure out how much garden space you'll need to feed your family.

Be on the lookout for our upcoming:

- Canning Timetable – Easy to use timetable for water bath and pressure canning at your elevation
- Companion Planting Guide – Say goodbye to plant eating pests by encouraging beneficial bugs in your garden.

Visit https://www.TheGreenHomesteader.com to get a link to your free downloadable content or scan the QR codes below.

Square Foot Garden Calculator

Budget Planner & SMART Goals Workbook

Introduction

Do you long to escape the rat race and move on to a simpler lifestyle? If so, then you are not alone. People from all around the country are tired of struggling with the high stress and unhealthy lifestyle associated with modern living. Consumerism is stacked on top of a pile of debt the size of Mount Everest. So many people put themselves through the ringer in search of true happiness when the answer is actually simple – quite literally.

Simpler living gets us back to the basics where we have more freedom, security, and control over our health. A lot of people want to achieve that dream. The problem is that only a handful of those people will ever take action. The rest will stay trapped in their stressful, highly processed, and pre-packed lifestyle, digging themselves into deeper debt.

The reason is because most people take the dream of a simple lifestyle and make it surprisingly complicated. It doesn't have to be that way. A simpler lifestyle is within everyone's reach, regardless of their current circumstances. Homesteading starts by making smarter choices that move you toward becoming self-sufficient. Many people begin the leap to homesteading from an apartment. If they can do it, then anyone can!

The key is to start small. Learn to cook, choose fresh produce over processed foods, grow a few plants, and spend money wisely. Start building a foundation for a simpler life and before you know it, you'll be living on your dream property enjoying a simpler life.

So, rather than dreaming of a simpler life, be one of the few who take action to achieve it.

Part 1

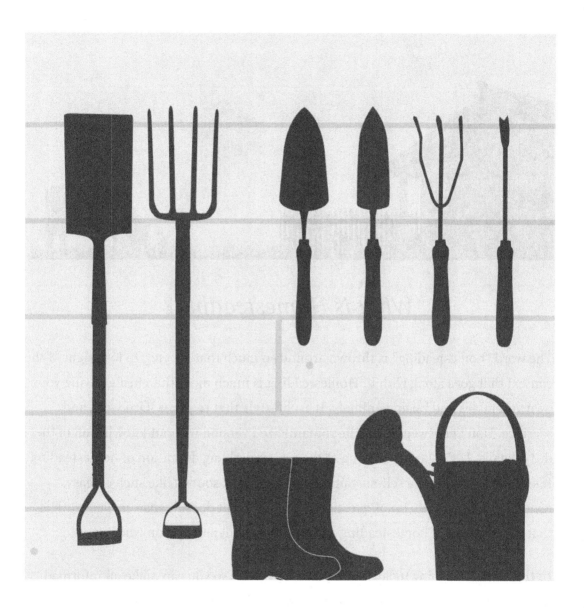

Homesteading Essentials

Chapter 1

What is Homesteading?

The word "homesteading" is thrown around so much that it's easy to lose sight of the context that goes along with it. Homesteading is much more than just growing your own vegetables and raising animals. It's a lifestyle that requires hard work and sacrifice. Don't get swept up in the romanticized version without knowing all of the dirty details. Let's start by looking at the real underlying definition of homesteading. It's the act of building a self-sustaining lifestyle. That sounds like such an easy concept but there are a lot of questions this statement doesn't answer. The truth is that the meaning of homesteading is a bit different depending on who you ask.

In this book, I'm going to lay out the cold hard facts so you can make an informed decision about whether or not homesteading is right for you. Sure, I could romanticize the hell out of this lifestyle. I carry family memories of working in my grandparents' garden. I spent my childhood climbing trees, surrounded by natural beauty while enjoying fresh afternoon snacks of apples, plums, and cherries that I purloined from the neighbor's fruit trees.

That's the expectation that most people have when they consider homesteading. It's all true but like a shiny coin found sitting in the mud, there's a dirty side – quite literally. Homesteading is built around hard work, dedication, and sacrifice. That's the price for enjoying the benefits of this lifestyle.

So, what exactly is homesteading? The truth is that homesteading is different for everyone. It can be anything from growing a garden to building a chicken coop in your own backyard. Unless you have a lot of extra cash to throw around, it usually starts as a small hobby that's cultivated into a lifestyle. Some people even start homesteading in suburban areas with very limited space, because at its core, homesteading is just creating a self-sufficient lifestyle. You can do that by growing a small garden on your balcony or investing in a large farm.

Anyone can start homesteading from anywhere in the world so don't let your current living situation stop you from pursuing your dream.

I think the question that should be asked is "What does homesteading mean to you?"

Let's find out!

Why Do People Homestead?

The image of homesteading you probably have in your head is of an individual settling on a large piece of land, donning their Davy Crocket coonskin hat, and hitting the fields with their rifle. That's because homesteading is associated with pioneering due to its origins in 1862.

The Homestead Act of 1862 was a law that stated all public land in the Western United States could be granted to any US citizen who was willing to live on and farm that land for at least 5 years. Of course, this law became obsolete in most states in 1976, but the point remains that many people still envision homesteading with this mental image.

Fast-forward to today's industrialized world and we see much of the population crammed into dense urban areas. We've seen two things happen over the past decade that have completely turned the world on its head. The first factor is the ever-increasing cost of food. But I think the one that's been the leading motivation for homesteading is all the studies being released about processed foods and just how much havoc they wreak on our bodies.

People are looking to break free of a system that exchanges health for convenience. The only way to achieve that is to become self-sufficient. The problem with giving up convenience is that, well, everything isn't convenient anymore. You don't just go into the chicken coop every day and gather eggs for breakfast. You have to feed and water the hens, clean the coop, fend off predators like raccoons and snakes, and dispose of ravaged poultry. All those dirty little tasks are done for you when you buy a dozen eggs from the grocery store but once you start homesteading, you have to do it all yourself. You also have to water the crops, add fertilizer, till fields, and do all the hard work that is already done for you when you step into the produce section of the grocery store.

Again, I'm not trying to scare you away from homesteading. I just want you to go into it with the right mindset. If you're expecting to just be able to walk through the coop every day to gather eggs or simply harvest crops every month of two, then you're going to be disappointed. All of the time spent in between gathering and harvesting is what defines homesteading. Those are also the things I absolutely love about it.

Everyone has their own reasons for homesteading. As a result, their expectations are also different. Sometimes retirement leads to a lack of aspiration, so homesteading is a way to fill the void left by a former career. Retirees may have the money to invest so they decide that becoming self-sufficient is a great way to stay busy. Others do it out of need when facing economic hardships and are looking to break the shackles that bind them to a soul crushing economy.

Every situation is unique, so as a homesteader you shape the land to meet those unique scenarios. Thus, no two homesteads look exactly alike as each one is cultivated through the dreams and aspirations of its creator. A homestead takes on the shape of its owner's unique vision and matches their goals.

Three Essential Homesteading Terms and Their Context

Homesteading can be broken down into three terms but in reality, there is a whole lot of context that goes behind these words.

- **Self-Sufficient:** "Needing no outside help in satisfying one's basic needs, especially with regard to the production of food."
- **Self-Reliant:** "Reliant on one's own powers and resources rather than those of others."
- **Sustainability:** This is an interesting concept. It means to support or maintain, but in modern times the definition is thought of in regards to natural resources leading to the following definition. "Avoidance of the depletion of natural resources in order to maintain an ecological balance." However, I like to think about it as a means of supporting and maintaining my family via a self-sufficient and self-reliant lifestyle.

Homesteading encompasses all three of those definitions. It's easy to get lost in the sea of complex definitions and varying opinions about homesteading but at the end of the day, it's broken down into those three basic categories.

So, using those terms, we can more easily define homesteading as developing a property with enough land to grow the crops and raise the livestock necessary to support your family. The size of the land only affects the percentage of your current lifestyle that you can make self-sustaining. A larger property may provide more freedom; however, it also comes at a higher financial and labor cost. But you don't have to start large. That's a huge misconception. We're going to focus on starting small and growing to the level that makes you happy. In short, you're creating a lifestyle that encompasses those three terms on a scale you find manageable

Depending upon your goals, homesteading generally involves one or more of the following:

- Growing your own food
- Preserving your own food
- Raising livestock
- Using renewable energy

Although, you don't have to adopt all of them. Even if you choose to only tackle one or two, you are essentially homesteading. This would technically be called contemporary or urban homesteading so let's take a closer look at this topic.

Homesteading in the Modern World

Contemporary homesteading is the label used to define the addition of renewable practices into a lifestyle. For instance, if you have a small property and decide to grow a tomato garden, then you would fall under the contemporary homesteading label.

It's broken down even further too with micro-steading, which would be someone deciding to grow a few plants on their balcony or the rooftop of an apartment building.

To get full blown homesteading, you would need a larger property with an abundance of crops and some livestock. If you're completely new to homesteading and have never worked on a farm, then you'll probably want to start with some form of micro-steading and work your way up.

The key is to find changes you can make right now in order to start steering your life toward homesteading. Don't get trapped in the moment waiting to buy a property or waiting for that perfect life to just find you. Inaction gets you nowhere. You can start your homesteading journey regardless of your current living situation. This is a point I'll drive home throughout this book.

My goal is to show you how to take small, achievable steps to build the life of your dreams. Together we're going to take the journey from modern living to homesteading one step at a time.

Chapter 2

Homesteaders, Preppers, and Survivalists

Homesteaders are often thrown under the same label as preppers and survivalists, but all three types of people have unique motivations that lead to different skillsets. If you heard that your uncle was a prepper, you'd probably expect to find a basement full of MREs, dry food, canned goods, and large barrels of water. This expectation could be right on the money, too. If that were true, your uncle would be a prepper who is prepared for an extreme scenario. Most preppers don't fall under this category though.

Labels like these are based on expectations. They are generally unreliable and lead to the wrong conclusion. Reality is often shaped by motivation. In the example above, the motivation for the Uncle would be preparing for society to completely fail. This is what we call a doomsday prepper. In reality though, if we were to face a doomsday scenario, having a basement full of supplies probably wouldn't be enough.

I only bring up such an extreme scenario to make one very important point. Wad up every preconception you have about preppers, survivalists, and homesteaders and throw them in the recycling bin. Reality paints a much different picture. Motivation is what defines the type of homesteader, prepper, and survivalist so that's what we'll focus on in this chapter.

I didn't start a homestead because I want to live through a doomsday scenario seeing the fall of society. Chances are that you don't want to see that either. We're both here to escape the crushing weight of a modern society that sets us up to fail. Money, health, and sanity are all pushed to the limit every day. Homesteading provides us an escape from the rat race and allows us to reap the rewards of our efforts in a way not possible when working for a large corporation.

Imagine you work in an office and spend your day entering information into a database, the task is never ending, there's always more data to input, and while that information is important to the company, you never really get to see the results of all your hard work.

Now imagine you spend your day working on the homestead. You've planted a garden, built a chicken coop and filled it with laying hens, and bought a dairy goat, which you milk every day. Now, every time you prepare a meal for your family, you get to appreciate the abundance of your efforts.

Just to be clear, escaping doesn't mean that you must completely abandon society. Homesteading is about gaining a new type of independence. We are still part of the community, but the difference is that we're not completely dependent on it either.

Homesteaders gain independence by cultivating skills used by both preppers and survivalists. We evolve them into a lifestyle that allows us to build a self-sufficient life.

What is a Prepper?

People who take extra steps to prepare for emergency situations are labeled as preppers. Most people envision preppers buying up supplies and hoarding them in a bomb shelter waiting for shit to hit the fan. However, prepping falls into a lot of different categories.

Families in Florida build Hurricane Kits to prepare for weeks without power just in case they get blasted by a powerful storm. Those living in the Mid-West have tornado shelters stocked with supplies just in case they find themselves in the path of a disastrous tornado. Californians have a planned evacuation kit in case fire forces them to leave their home immediately.

All the individuals listed above would be considered preppers. In short, a prepper is someone who prepares for emergency situations. With that said, homestead preppers are those who prepare for economic hardships by building a self-sustaining ecosystem that supports their lifestyle.

There are actually two types of preppers – disaster and preventative – each defined by their motivation. Disaster preppers are often incorrectly clumped up with survivalists. All the examples I described above would be considered disaster preppers. Doomsday disaster preppers tend to take it to a whole new level by preparing for a day when the economy fails and food chains that people so conveniently rely on fall apart.

The other category of prepper is preventative in nature. They plan their future much more logically and carefully, anticipating disaster and doing everything they can to prevent it. They build an environmentally friendly lifestyle, recycle, and do their part to live as green as possible. Installing solar panels, recycling, and eliminating use of plastic are all forms of preventative prepping.

A Prepper's Motivation

Preppers are motivated by a lot of factors and come in all different sizes. Covid-19 even left us with a whole new brand of prepper too – the pandemic prepper. Most people who decide to prep aren't under living a paranoid lifestyle that spells doom and gloom. They are just being reasonable. The fact is that disaster always hits when we least expect it, so preppers just make sure they're able to weather the storm.

The recent pandemic hit a lot of people with a serious dose of much-needed reality. The fact is that the motto "Be Prepared" might be the best advice on the planet.

Here's a question for critics of preppers. Why not be prepared? What does it hurt to make sure you have the necessary supplies for emergencies?

There's no good answer because being prepared is just common sense.

What is a Survivalist?

If you've ever watched the show "Survivor," then you've seen an example of a survivalist. Sure, it's an overly dramatized version, but the general foundation of the show is about survival. Contestants on this show are dropped on an island where they are forced to use everything around them to build homes, hunt food, and create a small community.

Whereas preppers focus on storing the resources to survive for long periods of time, survivalists develop the skills to live off the land indefinitely.

I'm sure you've heard the proverb, "Give a man a fish, and you feed him for a day. Teach a man to fish, and you feed him for a lifetime."

A survivalist in the proverb is the one who learns how to fish. If you learn to fish, then you can catch your own fish and not go hungry, even if society falls apart. The same is true for growing your own food, gathering your own water, and hunting animals.

Using that same proverb, a prepper would take a fish given to them and store it for later. A survivalist learns to fish so they can just hit the waters whenever they want.

Survivalist Motivation

Most survivalists aren't trying to live out some sort of doomsday scenario. The fact is that the majority of them simply love activities like hunting, fishing, and spending time in the wilderness. It's enjoyable and there's no better stress relief than spending quality time with Mother Nature herself.

Survivalists enjoy their ability to be self-sufficient and will spend days – sometimes weeks – in the wild. Some learn these skills out of necessity, like in the military. Others do it for sport.

At their core, survivalists are simply pursuing a hobby. Of course, you do have the doomsday people who are bragging about their survivor skills to their friends and family while bashing their lifestyle. These people don't make many friends though. Unfortunately, to the uneducated, this small group is how survivalists as a whole are seen.

Preppers and Survivalists and Homesteaders, Oh My

Many people use the three terms interchangeably. Preppers are seen as hoarders who are stockpiling goods and learning to survive in the event that society falls apart. This is partially right. Preppers stockpile but prepping in itself doesn't guarantee the ability to survive without a chain of supplies.

On the flip side, having survivalist skills doesn't inherently mean having the ability to stockpile goods. A survivalist knows how to survive in the wild without help but they don't necessarily stock up on supplies. They hunt when they're hungry and find water when they're thirsty.

Homesteaders learn to hunt, forage, and develop other skills to survive in the wild. Many of the skills you will develop operating your homestead from day-to-day will fall into this category. We draw on a survivalist mentality to learn these skills.

You will also learn to preserve food, which is a necessary prepping skill. You will budget time and food in a way that's going to leave you prepared to meet any challenges that life throws at you.

The fact is that having just one set of skills isn't enough. What happens if there's a storm that keeps you from hunting for several days? Our biology simply isn't cut out to survive that long without food. Sure, we can survive for weeks but the lack of nutrition would make us so weak that it would be extremely difficult to hunt or gather food.

Survivalists need prepping skills in order to reach their full potential. Now let's flip the coin and look at it from the other side.

Preppers who don't develop survivalist skills are still dependent on food supplies from outside sources. You can stock up a year's worth of food but if society were to fall apart, what would you do after that supply runs out? Without the ability to grow, hunt, and forage for your own food, you would still be at the mercy of outside influences.

Using the same proverb from earlier, we could say, "Give a man 365 fish and he eats for 365 days. Teach a man to fish and he eats for a lifetime."

The same proverb is just as true in that context.

Homesteading actually combines the two skillsets by drawing on their strengths. An expert homesteader will be able to grow and raise their own food while also possessing the skills to preserve it. They have the ability to adapt to major changes in society because of their self-sufficient approach. Homesteaders quickly become expert planners even if they didn't' start out that way. Through trial and experience, they identify their long-term and short-term needs and set goals to make sure they can meet them.

In short, homesteading combines the best of both worlds to give birth to a well-rounded skillset that's positioned to not only survive, but to thrive without being dependent on commerce. Self-reliance is the main motivation of a homesteader. We want to be free from our dependence on commerce and live a simpler life that won't be thrown out of balance when something happens.

Having skills from both survivalists and preppers is beneficial so I encourage you to ignore those who label them as extremists and start looking deeper. So now let's look at some of the key traits that define homesteaders and how you can use the skills in a unique way.

Chapter 3

Everyone Has Different Motivations

Motivation is what separates homesteaders from everyone else. We tend to draw our motivation from a mix of preppers and survivalists. It's not necessarily a fear of a cataclysmic event that motivates us to build a self-sufficient lifestyle. The motivation isn't that extreme. It's that we prefer a simpler life that is free from the shackles that lead to so much stress.

Preppers are motivated by their desire to be prepared for unexpected disasters, both man-made and naturally occurring. The goal is to have the supplies needed to survive through a breakdown of traditional services during an emergency.

Survivalists are generally motivated by their love of nature and love being in the wilderness. This connection with nature allows them to survive off the land for an extended period of time without the need for any traditional services.

Sure, there are extremists on every side whose motivations are based on paranoia and driven by fear. But most preppers and survivalists are not driven by these extremes. They are just following a lifestyle that makes them feel happier and more secure.

Lifestyle Choices Offer More Freedom

Many would be homesteaders choose this lifestyle to break free of the shackles that make so many people feel like slaves to a failing system. That's the vision anyway. But a lot of us tend to brilliantly merge a 21st century lifestyle with homesteading to give us even more freedom. Lifestyle is a major factor that defines homesteaders, preppers, and survivalists but you might not be able to spot these people in everyday life.

Your coworker in the cubical next to you might own several acres of farmland that she tends to after work. That manager who is routinely called "oblivious to challenges" could be spending his weekends in the wilderness hunting and foraging for food. Even your neighbor could have a years' worth of supplies packed into their basement.

In the 21st Century, you never know who could fall into one of these three categories. It's not that these people are completely giving up their lives in favor of some extreme lifestyle. They are simply exercising their right to choose their version of freedom during their off-hours.

Homesteading doesn't necessarily mean you have to drop your entire life, move to a large property, and completely cut yourself off from society. That's not really freedom. Most of us just want to live a more natural lifestyle where we know we're not dumping toxic processed food into our bodies. We want to be free of dependence on modern supply chains and processed foods to finally gain our independence. Since freedom comes in a lot of different forms, you'll need to define freedom for yourself.

In many ways, it's hard to identify homesteaders, preppers, and survivalists in a normal, 21st Century setting. Yet, so many people envision homesteading as moving off-the-grid and completely separating from society. That's not really homesteading though. Pioneers in the 1800s did not completely separate from society. They bartered, helped, and built their own social systems where everyone did their part.

What's the point of this whole sentiment? It's simple. Homesteading, prepping, and developing survivalist skills all create freedom by ensuring you can contribute even when supply chains fail like during the pandemic of 2021 when the grocery store aisles were bare. Homesteading separates you from dependency on franken-foods that lead to so many diseases today. More importantly, it gives you peace of mind.

Food Storage is a Defining Factor

Another way to contrast homesteaders and preppers is to look at how each of them store food. We already know that survivalists don't store food so they will be left out of this conversation.

With that in mind, preppers tend to use a more calculated approach to food storage. They sit down and do a lot of math to determine what supplies are needed over a specific timeframe. This timeframe is directly related to their motivation. Storm preppers might plan food storage for a month while more extreme motivations might lead preppers to plan for a year or longer.

Preppers then go to the store or visit an online commerce shop and buy those supplies. These goods are processed commercially.

Homesteaders also sit down to calculate their food storage, but their goal is to have enough supplies to last from harvest-to-harvest. Some supplies are bought commercially (toilet paper, paper towels, etc.) but food and water are grown and harvested on their property.

The exact ratio of commercial-to-naturally grown food stores depends on the homesteader's land usage and storage capacity. For instance, if they only grow one or two crops and have a few chicken coops, then they might have to purchase foods like powdered milk for storage.

Essentially, homesteaders are preppers focused on sustainability. If society were to completely fail, a prepper's stored supplies would run out within a year. Then what will they do? On the other hand, a homesteader would be able to continuously produce fresh food and water indefinitely.

Caring For Medicinal Needs

Homesteaders also bring together skills from both preppers and survivalists in order to care for their family's medical needs. Preppers store first aid supplies for the event that hospitals become unavailable. Survivalists learn about natural remedies that can be developed from plants which are easy to grow or forage in their area.

With homesteading, there is a balance of these two important skillsets. Storing first aid supplies is important for emergencies. But we also want to be self-sufficient so we learn about natural remedies that will treat or prevent most situations. While we don't go to the extremes that many preppers go through in terms of compiling a large list of supplies, we do have certain kits for emergencies.

Learning natural remedies is also a skill that I feel everyone should have. We've become so dependent as a society on the convenient over-the-counter remedies that we've lost touch with certain natural alternatives.

I'm not implying that you shouldn't visit the ER with a broken bone or seek medical attention if you're having a heart attack. The point I'm trying to drive home is that we can all benefit from learning basic natural remedies and first aid skills just in case they are needed. These remedies can be applied to yourself, your pets, and your livestock. I once treated a puppy with Parvo using chamomile, ginger, and peppermint tea to help him keep hydrated and reduce the nausea and vomiting so he could keep his food down. They are all soothing to the stomach and can be used in both humans and dogs. Thankfully this puppy survived and is doing well today.

Water Options for Homesteaders, Preppers, and Survivalists

Water is the number one necessity for all human life so it's safe to say that all preparedness plans must include access to water. You can have every other supply under the sun but if you don't have access to clean drinking water, then nothing else will really matter.

One of the first major steps that homesteaders take is to create sustainable water sources. This is done through wells, localized natural sources such as rivers and streams, and even building rainwater collection systems for watering crops and livestock.

Preppers find that water storage is what takes up the most space. As a rule of thumb, a person needs one gallon of water every day to be healthy. That means a prepper would need to store 365 gallons of water per person in order to prep for an entire year. That's a lot of H_2O!

Let's flip this to survivalists now. A survivalist learns how to find natural water sources and purify it using natural means. This usually involves boiling the water. Of course, there are other natural ways to purify water, like Solar Water Disinfection but survivalists tend to stick to the basics.

Homesteaders use important water habits from both preppers and survivalists in order to create sustainable water sources. Storage jugs can be distributed around the homestead to store large amounts of water. Just one 55-gallon barrel is enough to last one person nearly two months. Homesteaders also know how to purify water in the event it becomes necessary, but our main goal is to prevent us from having to do either.

A larger homestead should start with a well that has the option of swapping over to a manual pump and should also consider building a rainwater collection system for storing water for crops and livestock. These are two basics that every homestead should include and should be one of the first investments.

Adding in storage containers, jarring water, and other prep methods are entirely optional but not necessary.

Life Off-the-Grid

This is another area where a lot of people set completely unrealistic expectations. The perception of living completely "off-the-grid" is generally unrealistic in today's society. It's not impossible, but extremely difficult, so it's important to recognize that here's an enormous difference in living completely off-grid and building a lifestyle where you can live off-grid if shit hits the fan.

Homesteaders tend to take on a prepper's mentality and prepare for life off-the-grid if it becomes necessary. In essence, we work hard to lessen our dependence on public utilities. There are a lot of ways to achieve this too, which is what makes it so exciting.

Homesteaders usually have access to their own water and food at the very least. Additional newer technologies also exist that can keep a homestead operating without being supplied power from the grid as well. Wood stoves, propane heaters, and natural lighting are also a good idea.

Again, our goal is to grow into a self-sufficient lifestyle so that if the grid were to be completely cut off, we would still be able to thrive. We're using a prepper's mindset to create this self-sufficient approach just in case shit does hit the fan.

In the meantime, homesteaders can save a lot of money with an off-the-grid approach. By implementing solar and wind technologies as well as using geothermal techniques you can quickly start saving on heating and cooling costs associated with your local electrical utility.

Security of a Homestead

Homesteaders take steps to add security to their property and provide ways to defend it. Most protection comes from fences surrounding the property to protect livestock from natural predators, but this type is so obvious that I won't discuss it too much.

Thought should be given to protecting a homestead from the most dangerous predators of all – other humans! Extremists tend to stock up on guns, ammo, and other weaponry in order to prepare for a doomsday scenario where people are trying to take what doesn't belong to them. Here's the problem though. No hoard of guns will matter if there aren't enough people in your household to use them. So once again, homesteaders borrow from a prepper's skillset. They obtain and store enough guns and ammo for the number of people living in their home. Here's the important part though. You must teach everyone how to properly use the weapons. Hunting is a good survivalist skill that provides a ton of experience using weapons so it's highly recommended for homesteaders who arm themselves. If you are still uncertain, classes can often be found at your local shooting range. They vary from basic firearms safety to more advanced armed self-defense. Choose the option that best fits your needs and skill level.

Homesteaders Are a Breed of Our Own

The biggest downfall of both preppers and survivalists is that their skillsets are mostly geared to survive for a limited amount of time. When you break it down, they don't really have any long-term motivation. Preppers would have to go out and scavenge for supplies once their storage runs out and survivalists would have to hope that they find food and water every day.

As homesteaders, we think in the long-term. We don't look to the future to consider living off-the-grid. We look to the past to see how people thrived before the grid even existed. We plant the seeds from both lifestyles and grow them into something completely unique.

Preppers teach us how to ensure we have reserves to get through difficult times while survivalists teach us important hunting and foraging skills. But homesteaders create an ecosystem that thrives without a dependence on hunting or scavenging for supplies. We create it all ourselves.

What makes this lifestyle so beautiful is that we can do everything right now. We don't need to wait for a doomsday scenario that might not ever come to start living a self-sustaining lifestyle. Yet, we can still enjoy the fruits of our labor alongside modern society.

More importantly, homesteaders enjoy a lot of benefits such as lower long-term living costs and a simpler lifestyle that is free of the crushing stress of modern living. It is hard work, don't get me wrong, but it's the most rewarding experience I can imagine.

Chapter 4

The Homesteading Lifestyle

We live in a world of convenience, but that convenience is driven by an economy that always finds a way to throw a wrench into our plans. That's a hefty price tag! It's no wonder so many people seek independence. It also explains why homesteading has become such a popular topic in the past decade.

The problem is that we're bombarded with information from so many sources that it overwhelms us. I'm sure you've tried researching the basics of starting a homestead and are familiar with the hundreds of varying opinions lecturing about how great it is. All those benefits are lifted on a pedestal so high that it would give the Tower of Babel a run for its money.

The problem with building such a high pedestal is that without a solid foundation, all those aspirations crumble under the weight of unrealistic expectations and all your dreams come crashing back down to reality.

I'm not trying to scare you away from homesteading. In fact, all those benefits you've read about are real, tangible, and obtainable. The catch is that like all opportunities in life, each benefit comes with its own unique challenges. When you set your expectations too high, those challenges will topple the success you've achieved. That's why it's important to plan for every outcome and have realistic goals that allow you to be prepared for the difficulties you will have along the way.

There's no better time than today to start planning your new homesteading lifestyle. You'll begin by learning the basics and understanding the challenges of each benefit. For instance, homesteading delivers freedom from your reliance on commerce but it also challenges you to understand nature.

It's a Wonderful Life – The Many Benefits of Homesteading

Homesteading enriched my life in so many ways that it's impossible to list them all in a single chapter. Heck, I could write a whole book on the ways my life has been enriched by the simplicity of homesteading. My homestead is the peaceful release I need from the hectic nature of modern living. Yes, some of it is hard but when I sit down for a meal every evening, I have the peace of mind of knowing that everything was provided by my own two hands.

While homesteading is hard, dirty work it's also simple. I know exactly what I have to do every day. There are no office politics. There are no stressful deadlines from demanding clients. Okay, animals are demanding but that's a different story!

More importantly though, I have the security of knowing that the lifestyle I've chosen is sustainable. While I haven't completely abandoned modern living, if society were to fall apart today, I know that I would still be able to provide for my family. That's true peace of mind.

No matter your goals with homesteading, you can bask in the tremendous benefits that come hand-in-hand with this lifestyle. Sure, it's challenging but it's also one of the most rewarding experiences in the world.

Homesteading is a Healthy Lifestyle

It doesn't take a rocket scientist to deduce that homesteading is a healthy lifestyle. The convenience of modern living comes with a high cost that reaches far beyond finances. Processed foods, pollution from cities, and heavy stress are all costs that wreak havoc on health. Most people don't even realize how unhealthy their lifestyle is until they step away from it and onto their peaceful homestead.

Think about the last apple you ate and consider the journey it took to get into your hands. Consider how many people handled it from the time it left the tree and made it to the supermarket's produce section. On top of that, the apple was probably exposed to pesticides and picked before it was ripe which reduces its healthful properties.

Homesteading puts you in control of every single step of the growing process. From the time the seed is planted to the moment it's harvested, you know everything about that food. So obviously it's going to be healthier!

Of course, the health benefits of living on a homestead go far beyond the food going on the table. Homesteading involves a lot of physical activities. According to healthcare professionals, we all need at least 30 minutes of exercise every day. Homesteading lets you trade in that gym membership for some good old-fashioned work. Your home becomes the gym but rather than paying for membership, you are rewarded with the fruits of your labor.

In fact, the exercise you get tending to daily chores improves your cardiovascular health, reduces stress, and helps you maintain a healthy weight. Plus working on a homestead is much more rewarding than hitting the treadmill or pumping weights in the gym.

When you clean the chicken coop, you know that you'll be rewarded with eggs. Tending to crops will yield delicious vegetables in the end. Everything you do has a purpose.

Combining healthier homestead-sourced food and rewarding exercise naturally leads to a decreased risk of disease. One out of every three adults in the United States are obese.[i] Americans are loading their bodies with unhealthy foods and compounding that unhealthy habit with a lack of physical activities.

I stumbled across a neat study that links health and homesteading in a unique way. It revealed that people living in greener areas experience a substantial 41% lower death rate for kidney disease and a 34% drop in respiratory disease.[ii] In short, people who live in greener areas live longer. It's likely because of the lifestyle attached to the majority of people living in greener areas. The relaxing atmosphere and clean air of a homestead are simply unmatched.

Teach your Kids Responsibility

Life on the homestead is an amazing experience for kids. Depending on their age, they might be hesitant at first but once they see how much freedom a homestead gives them, they will quickly come around. In fact, homesteading is a wholesome family experience that teaches new skills, improves bonds, and teaches valuable life lessons. These lessons are no longer taught in modern schools and many homes. Most adults have long forgotten them too. Living a homesteading lifestyle will prepare children to become self-reliant whether they decide to homestead or pursue another lifestyle when they grow up, those skills will be with them for the rest of their lives.

Another benefit of homesteading is that children form bonds that aren't possible when living in the city. Children develop bonds with something other than their smartphones. They connect with their environment and form bonds with the animals they care for every day. Just be careful when letting your small children care for meat animals because they might talk you out of eating them!

Of course, children must eventually learn hard lessons about the circle of life which includes death. Children who bond with the environment become more aware of things like weather and wildlife. Those lessons instill true wisdom, and your children begin to truly understand how everything around them is intertwined. I cannot overemphasize just how beneficial it is to understand where the things you eat come from.

In short, your children gain skills that most adults in today's society don't have. Skills that will give them an edge, like the ability to solve problems without spending hours doing a Google search. Homesteads give you ample opportunities to face challenges and find creative ways to solve them. So, it doesn't matter what they decide to do with their lives, homesteading instills ideals and skills that carry over into pretty much every lifestyle.

With that said, the best thing children learn when growing up on a homestead is responsibility. In my opinion, personal responsibility is the most important trait a kid can learn growing up. It's also a trait we see a lot of people today lacking.

Growing up on a homestead kids have daily chores like filling water troughs, cleaning, and other normal activities. These chores teach kids the importance of managing their responsibilities. If they don't fill water troughs, then the animals will die. Sure, kids will make mistakes these moments will be life lessons, for example the death of an animal due to failing to close a pen. It's a difficult lesson that will have a long-term impact on the way they address future responsibilities.

The important lesson to learn is that there are consequences for not following through with their responsibilities. It paints life in an entirely different picture when you have the power of life and death in your hands and these lessons carry over into adulthood.

In my community, they have a Drive Your Tractor to School day. In larger suburban areas and cities, just the mere thought would be enough to send most people into a panic, but because we know the children in our area are taught responsibility from a young age, we celebrate their opportunity to be rewarded for their industriousness.

Best of all, you'll be able to work side-by-side with your child and teach them these important lessons. Hard work has a way of forming bonds. Everyday tasks will become opportunities to teach and bond with your children. Even if you opt against home schooling your children, the lessons learned on a homestead will compliment what they learn in school. After all, the most important lessons in life aren't learned in a classroom.

Homesteading Creates Wonderful Opportunities for Families to Bond

Homesteading provides unparalleled opportunities for family bonding. Working together to build a self-sustaining lifestyle will develop strong bonds that are next to impossible to break. You'll impart essential life skills to your children that follow them for the rest of their lives while growing closer to your spouse as you build a new life together. It's a truly incredible experience that I wouldn't trade for anything in the world.

For a homestead to be successful, the entire family has to play their part. You're a team that celebrates success together. Every new achievement is a family moment. At the same time, every setback is shared by everyone so you're never alone. You share the ups and downs that come with this lifestyle.

Nothing builds stronger bonds that teamwork which is why so many large corporations have team building activities. They are trying to capitalize on what your family is learning by just living. Most businesses don't have an environment conducive to being a team player, so they have to create the artificial environment. You are lucky that your environment allows the whole family to grow closer as they navigate daily life on the homestead. It's a truly rewarding experience that allows you to connect on a level that seems lost on so many people in today's fast-paced society.

Free Yourself from the Stress of Modern Living

Getting away from the hustle of city life is one of the biggest stress reliefs under the sun. While life on a homestead certainly comes with its own set of unique challenges, it's also salvation from the mental and emotional stressors that come with city life. Most people don't even realize the negative trauma they are enduring while living in the city. Traffic is always clogging the streets, crowd-fighting is a common event, and you're always breathing in polluted air.

The constant bombardment of ever-present stimuli generates negative emotion that slowly builds over time. It's a large reason we're seeing an all-time decline in mental health. In short, city life slowly grinds away at your emotional health. By escaping that grind and returning to a simpler life, you regain control over your mental health.

Is homesteading really less stressful than city life? Well, I certainly won't tell you that it's easy. It's simple, sure. After all, you have a list of tasks that need to be done daily and you carry them out. Many of those tasks require manual labor, which I would never call "easy."

Running a homestead in the country provides an escape from the stress that accompanies city living. It's detox for your senses. You won't have noise pollution overwhelming your hearing or smog polluting your lungs. It's a simple lifestyle where you wake up and spend your time carrying out specific tasks. You won't have to fight crowds or stare at a computer screen for hours at a time.

Your time will be spent with Mother Nature. Humans thrive in nature. In fact, studies back up this claim. Spending time in nature lowers blood pressure, muscle tension, and improves heart rate. It also lowers the production of stress hormones.

In summary, city living overwhelms your senses and everyday life keeps adding to a compounding inner stress. Separating from the city by homesteading not only removes you from this environment, but also connects you with nature. You are removing stress from your life and adding in activities that also reduce stress. It's a powerful combination.

With that said, stress isn't the only healthy benefit of life on the homestead so let's shed some light on other health benefits associated with this amazing lifestyle.

Declare Financial Freedom

In the modern world, success is seen as "having a job" and making as much money as possible. We're forced to live in a society where status is dictated by the size of our bank account. Everything is conveniently found in stores and shops around the world, assuming you have the money to pay for it. Having the ability to buy everything you need is called financial freedom, but is freedom really the right word?

Yes, we can survive and thrive in a world of convenience but here's the part everyone leaves out. That freedom only applies if you have a high paying job and are willing to put up with the stress of a modern lifestyle. In fact, most people don't really feel free at all. They are trapped in dead-end jobs, forced to live in a cramped apartment, crushed by a mountain of debt and the competition of consumerism.

It sure doesn't feel like freedom. The truth is that life doesn't have to be that crushing. You don't have to trade your freedom for convenience. You can actually have both.

Homesteading offers true independence by building a life that's self-sufficient. We're not forced to endure harsh food prices and growing interest rates. If you enjoy some of the conveniences of modern living, then that's okay! Homesteading isn't about giving up the conveniences of modern living and becoming a hermit living on a large property devoid of all societal contact. Convenience is a great benefit until you become dependent on it. Homesteading breaks that dependence.

Homesteading allows you to gain true financial freedom because you're not dependent on commerce to meet your basic needs. Over time, you can become debt-free, and your utilities will be next to nothing if you scale your homestead appropriately.

Here's the part that I find ironic though. A lot of homesteaders have incomes considered to be below the Federal poverty line. Yet, they eat like Kings and have an over-abundance of stored supplies. Their property is loaded with natural resources. In fact, when you dig down deep, they have more than many "middle class" citizens working full-time jobs. It's pretty wild to think about it.

Foster a Sense of Community

One of the biggest misconceptions about homesteaders is the idea that we lock ourselves down on a property in the middle of nowhere and hide away from society. Although I'm sure there are a few exceptions, we're not hermits. The goal isn't to completely separate from society. It's to live independently from it.

Community is important to homesteaders. If you've ever been to a small farming town, then you know just how tight knit these communities are. They come together during a crisis, sharing in the good times, and working together to survive the tough times. It's a one-of-a-kind experience.

There's no cutthroat competition between homesteaders. Okay. Maybe a few friendly rivalries but that's about it. If Joe down the street discovers a better technique for getting higher crop yields, he doesn't keep it a secret. In fact, he'll eagerly tell everyone who'll listen!

Homesteading builds strong community bonds that have been lost in the modern lifestyle. I'm probably biased but I believe that the homesteading community is one of the strongest and most generous communities in the world. In fact, a strong community spirit is at the heart of homesteading. The attitude of the homesteading community is simple, but profound. When homesteaders have an over-abundance, they tend to give to other homesteaders who aren't so fortunate. There's no expectation of "returning the favor."

Of course, no community is perfect. There are conflicts and miscommunication. And small towns have a reputation for gossiping way too much. But that's just human nature. It's the overall attitude that makes homesteading the greatest community in the world.

Chapter 5

Things I Wish I Knew Before I Started

It's easy to get swept up in the excitement of the homesteading dream. Self-sufficiency and living off-the-grid are both incredibly appealing lifestyles for so many people, but the reality isn't quite so clean-cut. When my family decided to adopt this lifestyle, we were just as excited as I'm sure you are while reading this. We rushed in and got our hands dirty as quickly as possible. Sounds like the best approach, right?

Well yes and no. We made a ton of mistakes that upon reflection leave us scratching our heads. I often ask myself "What were we thinking?"

While I'm all for bypassing procrastination in favor of the headfirst approach, there are some things that are worth learning before banging your head against the wall. We spent a lot of time during our second year fixing mistakes we made during our first year when we should have just taken the time to learn.

It's okay to make some mistakes along the way. That's healthy and normal. But just try to avoid mistakes that are going to cost you thousands of dollars in repairs and weeks of crippling stress.

I'm hoping to help you save money and prevent stress by sharing some of my early frustrating, head scratching mistakes. Ideally, I'd like to show you how to avoid them altogether.

The Reality of Off-The-Grid Living

Becoming energy independent is quite appealing but the reality is much different than many people envision. The first lesson is that we live in a society where it's nearly impossible to be completely removed from the grid. Depending on local regulations and laws, there might be permits and other legal requirements you must meet. Plus, the technology behind off-the-grid energy is quite extensive and has a steep learning curve.

Let's start by looking at the three biggest mistakes that often victimize the intrepid homesteader.

Not Enough Knowledge About Off-The-Grid Utility Systems

There are a lot of components that are used in our everyday lives that many of us never give a second thought, until we've been sitting in the dark for hours waiting for the lights to come on. Off-the-grid living is different. Without the proper setup, you could find yourself sitting in the dark all night in the crippling cold with only a blanket to keep you warm.

Solar power is great, but it's also expensive to install. You might not have access to it right away. In that case, you probably want to keep the electricity on, so your family is healthy. But you can install a wood furnace for heat and use candles for light in some scenarios.

Avoid rushing into this lifestyle without a plan. Consider all your family's activities and install renewable energy systems that meet those basic requirements. The easiest place to start is a wood burning stove and heater.

In the meantime, thoroughly research other options and learn as much as you can. Solar panels are a great long-term goal that will lead to independence. But do you know how battery banks work or how many panels you'll need to meet your basic needs?

Again, research this thoroughly while making small changes right now to cut energy usage. But don't separate from the grid until you are absolutely sure your home is 100% sustainable.

Don't Waste Energy

Most of us are raised without learning energy efficiency. We're just so used to having unlimited energy that it never crosses our mind to save until we start getting expensive electricity bills. Homesteaders don't have the luxury of unlimited energy – not if we want to live off-the-grid. Every watt of power must be carefully planned and never wasted.

Start developing the proper habits right now. The first is to use natural lighting during the day and keep the indoor lights turned off. Open the curtains and let as much sunlight as possible into your home. Another one is to invest in a wood heater and a wood stove. Both are affordable and will substantially cut your power costs.

The biggest thing is to prioritize your energy usage. Make a list of things you need electricity for and then try to cut back all other areas. For instance, do you really need an electric coffee maker, or can you use a percolator to save energy? Is that food mixer really necessary when you can mix by hand? I'm not saying you can't use either of those things, but just be aware of the power they require. Even small appliances add up over time.

Install a Reliable Water Source

With all of the talk of energy, it's easy to miss out on the most important element of all – water. Ensure that you have a water source that's reliable. In most cases, you can have a deep well installed but keep in mind that this costs a lot of money. Plus, if you opt for a well, then make sure you have a hand pump installed along with the electric pump so that you can cut back on energy usage and have a backup option.

When we purchased our property, we were truly excited that the previous owner had installed a well. What we didn't know was that it was a sulfur well and that the seller had failed multiple times in finding a water purification process that could mitigate the hard sulfur water. And unfortunately, the 5-acre orchard we planted our first year was vulnerable to sulfur, so in the end, we couldn't use the well water. We had to water by hand. This is a good time to remind you all to do your due diligence when purchasing a forever property.

For watering gardens and food crops that are being produced on a mass scale, try using a rainwater collection system so you are not pulling water from your drinking source. Or if there is a pond or lake on your property, then consider installing an irrigation system using that source. Because we were unable to use our well, we are planning to put in an irrigation system that relies on the stream at the back of our property.

Some homesteaders opt to install purification systems and use a lake or pond for drinking water. However, I don't recommend that for two reasons. The first is that we live in an industrialized world where contaminants often find themselves washing into local water sources. No purification system can protect against every possible unnatural contaminant, and you don't want to put your family's health at risk.

The other reason is that droughts happen and will quickly dry up standing water sources. While these are great sources for irrigation, don't depend on them for your family's survival. A well is the best choice if they are viable in your area.

Familiarize Yourself with Local Laws

Just because you own a property doesn't always mean you can do whatever you want with it. Areas have very specific zoning laws that you must follow. This is true even if you don't have neighbors.

Remember, everything you build must be done according to specific codes. These codes change depending on where you live so it's important that you research this thoroughly beforehand. In fact, don't buy a property until you have made sure you're actually allowed to install the items required for homesteading.

Even things you'd consider mundane and ordinary often require a permit. This includes installing a well or solar panels. Barns, green houses, and even chicken coops sometimes require specific permits. Some places won't even let you own farm animals.

Don't wait until you've already dropped the money on a down payment before discovering this important information.

Also be aware of deed restrictions. While your city or county may allow certain activities on your property, your deed may have its own set of restrictions. Case in point, while our property is quite rural, our deed does not allow for commercial poultry or swine farms. Additionally, there are restrictions against single wide mobile homes. Fortunately, neither of these was an issue for us, but if we did have aspirations for raising pigs commercially, we would have been sorely disappointed.

The Three Biggest Setbacks of Homesteading

Choosing the Wrong Location

I truly believe that the homesteading lifestyle can be done no matter where you live. Even apartment dwellers can find ways to adopt certain portions of this lifestyle. With that said, investing in a property is such a big step that you need to do your homework. We just looked at how zoning laws are different depending on the location of the property. Make absolutely sure that the local laws are friendly to homesteaders.

Of course, choosing the right location goes beyond legalities. Do a walkthrough of the property before agreeing to buy it. Pay close attention to elevation and look for signs of previous flooding. Don't wait until you've moved there and planted a garden to discover that the property is prone to flooding. That would be a costly mistake.

We had considered putting tiny vacation cabins on our property near the river and found out the first spring that our little cabins might have floated away because the flood maps were incorrect. If flooding is prevalent on the property, consider talking to some of the neighbors who've been around awhile. I find that they are always happy to talk about their home.

You can begin by making a list of everything that your property must have and don't settle for anything that doesn't meet those requirements. You might have to wait a bit longer for something to open up, but I promise it's worth the wait. We spent more than two years looking for just the right property and are so happy we didn't settle.

It's also important to never rely on your realtor to tell you everything. Chances are that they don't have all of the information. Seller's will often hide defects to get a quick sale. But a few quick calls and internet searches can show you a ton of information about any property. This is the biggest investment of your life so it's important that you get it right.

Trying to Do Too Much, Too Fast

Homesteading has a pretty steep learning curve so it's absolutely imperative that you take it one step at a time. This is easier said than done though. Just like everything in life, a new venture starts with excitement and enthusiasm. This often causes us to take on more than we can handle. Don't make this mistake.

You will have a seemingly endless number of projects that must be done. When you try to do too many things at once, you end up rushing through those projects because you feel a sense of urgency. For instance, we had to rebuild our fence because we rushed to build it in the beginning and got it wrong. That was a costly mistake that could have easily been avoided had we given ourselves adequate time to properly build it the first time.

The best approach is to focus on a single project at a time. Finish it completely before moving onto the next. Don't try to juggle multiple projects at the same time. Make a list of projects that need to be completed and rank them according to their priority. Then tackle them individually rather than at the same time.

Not Planning Properly

Starting a homestead is an exciting time so it's easy to get swept up in the moment. But jumping in without a plan is a bad idea. I'm not saying that you should research for years without taking action. There's a fine line between thoroughness and procrastination. Eventually, you have to dive into these unknown waters.

Keep in mind that you can adjust your plan later down the road as you gain experience. A basic homesteading plan includes:

- Goals
- Finances
- Animals you plan to raise
- Crops you plan to grow
- Items needed to meet the above requirements

If you fail to lay out a basic plan, you'll end up with resources you'll never use or you'll buy the wrong property. Just don't get so caught up in research that you never take action.

Remember, the basic plan is just the beginning. Your plan will grow and change as your skills and knowledge grow. For now, just implement the basics and build upon it.

Other Common Homesteading Mistakes

Not Understanding the Basics of Gardening

Most of us are not born with a green thumb. It's a skill we learn and develop through experience. If you're going to create a self-sustaining farm, then you have to learn much more than just the basics of gardening.

Certain plants thrive next to each other while others will literally choke each other out. You also need to understand what crops grow best at certain times of the year, so your garden has plants growing for as many months as possible. This depends on your climate and location.

At the very least, learn when to plant specific crops and whether or not they can be grown as neighbors. I recommend that you sketch a gardening map so that you have a plan moving forward. Once you know the exact plants you'll be growing, then you can study up on them to learn more about their care.

Overestimating Your Abilities

The concept of homesteading seems simple when reading about it online, but the reality is this lifestyle is quite rigorous. Don't fall prey to the idea that homesteading is going to be all fun and games. Building a self-sufficient life requires a lot of hard work, manual labor, and perseverance.

Furthermore, you must learn a lot of different skills to be successful. Gardening, animal husbandry, carpentry, and landscaping are just a few of the dozens of skills required to run a homestead.

You must have the right mindset going into this process or else it will crush you. Go into it knowing that it will be difficult and don't overestimate your abilities.

Forgetting to Enjoy Life

It's easy to get swept away by the work of running a homestead. It can be stressful to both the mind and body if you forget to stop and enjoy life. Many new homesteaders forget why they started their homestead in the first place – for a simpler more enjoyable life. Well, if you're not stopping to enjoy life, then what's the point of homesteading? Why not stop and smell the roses when you can?

Spend time enjoying family meals together eating food provided by your own two hands. Read a book on those rainy days when you can't do a lot of outside work. Enjoy time with your kids. Don't get so caught up in the work that you forget about the joys of living.

Part 2

Finding your Reason

Chapter 6

Is Homesteading for Me?

Before you invest thousands in purchasing a new homestead property to begin your new journey, make sure it's the right lifestyle for you and your family. Becoming a full-time homesteader, or even more, running a massive self-sustaining homestead like Joel Salatin, is a full-time commitment and not something that can be done halfway. Be sure you are prepared before you jump in headfirst. There are lots of mistakes you can make that will break the bank if you don't do proper research and planning.

I highly encourage you to start slowly and take on a few small homesteading responsibilities before you make a final decision. Luckily, you can take on small homesteading tasks wherever you live!

We've talked about the benefits of homesteading and now we need to find your reason for homesteading, then find activities that match those reasons. For instance, if your reason is to eat healthier, then growing crops will be a primary objective of your homestead. In that case, you'll start a small garden, tend to it, and follow through with the daily responsibilities that it entails.

Next, consider all of the daily activities that your primary objective will require. Write them down, read through the list several times and make sure you're willing to commit to those tasks.

Visit my website at www.TheGreenHomesteader.com to get your free bonus budgeting and SMART goal-setting workbook to jumpstart your journey.

If you're married and/or have children, you have to make sure they are 100% committed as well. Do their goals align with yours? If not, you might need to adjust the plan. If your spouse isn't committed to homesteading, then you'll have a difficult time living this lifestyle. Everyone on a homestead must contribute in some way in order to meet the needs of the entire household.

Once you're decided that you're willing to do everything on the list, then you're halfway there. But you've only committed on paper. That's not enough. Real life experience is the only way you'll know for certain so let's look at a few small steps you can take to gain real life homesteading experience.

Step 1: Do Your Homework

YouTube is a great tool for seeing homesteading in action. I encourage you to watch several hours of video detailing the homesteading tasks you'll need to carry out before making any decisions. Seeing it with your own eyes provides insight into these tasks and will ensure that you're truly committed to this lifestyle. If watching a video of these tasks is too demanding, then consider that actually carrying out the tasks will be ten times more demanding.

You can also watch documentaries from homesteaders to gain some insight into their lifestyle. Just keep in mind that many of these documentaries only show you the positive sides of this lifestyle. What you want to see are the dirty details. For instance, if the person is clean after tending to their crops, chances are that you're not seeing the whole picture.

Finally, you can join a few homesteading forums and Facebook groups, such as The Green Homesteader, to connect with other homesteaders. They will answer questions and tell you what to expect.

Step 2: Create a Few Small Goals

If you made it through the previous step and are still willing to commit to homesteading, it's time to set a few small goals. Each goal should be something you can achieve while living at your current residence.

The fact is that you can practice homesteading from practically anywhere. Even an apartment with a balcony gives you a place to garden, although you'll be quite limited. Still, it's enough to gain some practical experience.

For every reason on your list, set a specific goal that you can achieve right now. Here are a few examples:

- If the goal is eating healthier, then start limiting your grocery list to items that can be produced on a homestead. After all, you won't find processed foods on a homestead!
- If the goal is to live a greener life, then find ways to reduce your carbon footprint right now. There's no reason to wait! List a few changes you can make to reduce your carbon footprint.
- What will you do on the homestead? What food do you plan on growing? What kinds of animals will you raise?

Step 3: Implement the Changes

The truth is that you don't have to wait until you're living on your dream homestead to start the lifestyle. You can make small changes right now that will get you into the groove. Even apartment dwellers are able to take steps toward homesteading.

The idea is to become self-sufficient. If you have a sunny window or a balcony, then grow a couple of plants just so you can gain some small bit of experience into the lifestyle required. Those with a larger backyard can grow entire gardens.

Start recycling if your primary goal is to live a greener life. Take the stairs instead of the elevator since it conserves power and improves your fitness level for when you have to do the manual labor on the farm. These small steps help you cement your reason for homesteading.

Step 4: Solidify your Reason

Once you've followed through with all of the steps above, it's time to commit to your reason. While it's possible to have multiple motivations for homesteading, make one of them a priority and focus mainly on that one.

Be absolutely sure you're ready to commit to your reason. If it's half-hearted, then the hard work is going to beat you down. It's like trying to drive a nail with only half a hammer. You'll get nowhere.

Analysis Paralysis

Planning and analysis are wonderful but eventually, you have to commit to it. Don't wait for some magical moment to commit. Do it right now. There's nothing holding you back from building a self-sufficient lifestyle.

We're going to look at the most powerful reasons for starting a homestead and discuss them in detail. I'll share the challenges and even give you a few tips for getting started right away, no matter where you live.

I'll be blunt. People who make excuses never achieve anything. There are always going to be reasons not to start. What if our forefathers had said, "Well we can't sign a Declaration of Independence right now because we don't have an army large enough to win."

Declare your independence and take action starting right now.

Reason #1: Declare Financial Freedom

The idea of signing off on your independence and exiting the rat race is an appealing thought. Everyone who has considered homesteading has played this scenario out in their mind at least once. Looking at the rising price of food and daydreaming of freedom from this insanity is a desire shared by a lot of aspiring homesteaders.

Homesteading does deliver on the promise of financial freedom but only if you plan accordingly. Those who leap headfirst into homesteading without a plan often find themselves crushed with debt, emotionally broken, and always on the verge of losing everything.

That's why it's so important to have a financial plan for starting your homestead. The costs are often underestimated and end up blindsiding families who impetuously dive into the process. Don't fall prey to the same mistakes that have plagued the dreams of so many aspiring homesteaders.

The Costs of Starting a Homestead are a Challenge to Overcome

A large part of people's budget is dedicated to things like rent or mortgage, credit cards, student loans, utilities, and other necessities. These debts weigh us all down to the point where we feel like change is impossible. So, the first challenge you'll meet is finding a way to budget in the money for homesteading while still juggling all of these other obligations.

As the famous proverb states, every journey begins with a single step. So, the first step here is to understand the costs associated with starting a homestead. Remember, The Green Homesteader website has bonus materials to help you get started.

The primary expenses of a homestead are land costs, animals, and infrastructure. Each of these branches into other costs but those three are the primary categories. Learning to stick to a strict budget will help you plan for each of those expenses.

Declare Financial Freedom Right Now!

Financial freedom is disguised as an undefeatable beast that blocks the path to all of our hopes and dreams. But it's really all bark and no bite. Financial freedom is the most straight-forward task on this list. The problem is that lenders have spent billions convincing you that it's impossible to get out of debt without applying more debt. It's a vicious cycle that you must end right now if you want to build a new life.

So why is financial freedom such a straight-forward path? Because it's actually an easy concept to follow. Right now, chances are that you're spending a ton of money on things that you don't need. How many people pay $10 for a cup of coffee and then complain that it's impossible to get out of debt?

The concept is this: Stop wasting money on frivolous expenses. You don't need the newest phone or the trendy clothes. I'm not saying to get rid of your phone. But there's a huge difference in paying $1,000 for that new iPhone and spending $100 on an older model – a $900 difference to be exact. Imagine what you could do with $900! And that's just one example!

Sit down, grab your notebook, or the budget planner you printed from The Green Homesteader website, and write down all of your necessary expenses. Start by listing the essentials like rent, electricity, water, food, insurance, car payment, gas, and maybe internet if you consider it essential.

Now write down all non-essential expenses. This includes things like Netflix, cable, gym memberships, and other items that are not essential to living. If you are using the workbook, you can circle these items to remove them from your total.

Now it's time to grab your calculator and do a little math. Take your income and divide it into three sections as follows:

- 50% of income
- 30% of income
- 20% of income

Here's how the 50/30/20 rule works. 50% of your income should be dedicated to essential living expenses. 30% of your income should be for non-essential expenses. 20% should either be put into a savings account or used to pay off debt.

I've developed a planning workbook that you can get for free by visiting https://www.TheGreenHomesteader.com and sending a request. This free gift is a thank you for supporting The Green Homesteader.

The next step is to cut and trim as much as possible right now to meet those criteria. Non-essential costs can simply be cut since you don't need them. However, if your living expenses are higher than 50%, that's where things get tricky. You can balance your budget differently, but I recommend you start by trying to find ways to cut those costs.

For instance, you can usually call around to get lower insurance premiums or even pay it annually for a substantial savings. You might be able to shop wiser at the grocery store to save some money on food. And if food costs are really high in your area, try looking into cost sharing by buying in bulk with friends and family. Most people can get their living expenses to under 50% of their income. It just requires a bit more planning.

This is a small step and doesn't require a whole lot of work. Plus, there's absolutely no excuse for not having a budget. Here are some additional tips:

- Pay off Highest Interest Rate Debt First.
- Consider cutting into your Non-Essential Budget to Pay off Debt Faster. Paying more than the minimum payment on your high interest debt can significantly reduce the amount of interest you pay overtime.
- Set up 20% of your Income to be Directly Deposited into Savings.
- Take Care of your Property. Better care equals longer lifespan and less money on replacement and/or repair.
- Live Below your Means.
- Develop a Minimalist Mindset.

Reason #2: Provide your Own Food

Food comes with a hefty price tag but many of the costs are not even related to finances. The price tag I'm referring to is not financial. In fact, the average cost of food in the US is one of the lowest in the world at face value but there are a ton of added costs that are paid later in life.

One of the most appealing aspects of breaking the shackles of supply chain dependence is that it gives you access to healthier food. Unless you're buying from the local Farmer's Market, the food you eat right now is severely lacking in nutritional value.

Home grown food is miles better than anything you'll find in the grocery store, including foods labeled as completely organic. Even organic produce is picked before it fully ripens to make the long trek to the produce aisle which reduces the available nutrients[iii].

A lot of people take supplements to offset the nutritional deficiencies that come with the average consumer lifestyle. Foods that you grow yourself are dense in nutrients and taste better than anything you can find in the grocery store.

Nutritional value aside, the act of gardening itself boosts both physical and mental health.

The True Cost of Convenience

Industrialized food has created a society where we no longer have to depend on hunting and gathering. We can just go to the store and buy what we want. In a sense, this seems like a much more secure lifestyle, but this security carries a hefty price tag.

Society as a whole has become short-sighted, and convenience minded. Most people don't understand the true nature of the food they're eating. They understand that what they want is found on Aisle five but everything before that is a blank filled in by preconceived notions and misbeliefs. How many people consider that the tomato that just went into their salad has spent the majority of its life sprinkled by poisonous pesticides? What about that turkey you had on Thanksgiving? Unless it's organic, it was probably pumped full of steroids and antibiotics until just days before being killed.

Sure, people love to echo fancy labels like "organic" and "grass fed" but how many of them truly understand what those labels mean? For instance, foods labeled as organic are certified to use only natural processes, but they still don't have the same nutritional value as food you would grow on a homestead.

Homesteading brings us all closer to the food that goes on our table, so we understand its complete cycle. You will have helped it thrive, nurtured it, and have been responsible for every moment of its growth so you know what's going on your table.

There are other hidden costs too, such as the food supply's dependence on fossil fuels that could skyrocket at any given moment. In fact, we're seeing that happen right before our very eyes in 2022.

We haven't even gotten to the environmental costs of agriculture. Fertilizer runoff, nitrogen fertilizers, and massive amounts of farming land being lost to erosion. These are high costs that are being charged to the future which are avoidable when you use sustainable agricultural practices.

Reason #3: Lead a Healthier Lifestyle

One of the biggest drawbacks of modern living is that it's not exactly the healthiest lifestyle. The hustle of working at stressful corporate jobs just to scrape by leads to a lot of emotional trauma that compounds over time. Even just the fact of living in a cramped city is unhealthy. In fact, according to the World Health Organization

[(WHO)](), 99% of people are breathing unhealthy air. Also factor in the unhealthy foods we just discussed, and you end up with a trifecta of poor health factors that are slowly draining your life and sanity from you.

Many homesteaders choose this lifestyle to escape the hustle and bustle of city life. They feel the unending drain it's taking on their body and mind, so they opt for a healthier lifestyle. This is great motivation. Of course, we all define health a bit differently so it's important to set clear goals if you choose this as your reason.

Eating whole foods grown on the homestead is definitely a good starting point for being healthy, but the physical activity on the farm is better exercise than anything you'll find at the gym. Plus, unlike a gym membership where you have to pay for your health, you are rewarded for your work on the homestead!

The connection between homesteading and health doesn't stop at exercise and healthier eating either. Your mental health will also benefit from living away from the city. Respiratory health is vastly improved since you won't be forced to breathe pollution every day. Also, the sunshine you enjoy while doing manual labor on a farm gives your body essential Vitamin D.

What makes homesteading such a powerful health boost runs much deeper than anything we've discussed so far. After all, you can technically gain all of those health benefits in other ways. But the one thing you absolutely cannot fabricate is the deeper purpose that homesteading provides.

Yes, you can follow a strict diet and be healthier. You can exercise every day at a gym and be healthier. But both of those are mindless tasks that don't give you the one thing that all humans crave above all else – a sense of purpose. When you find purpose to your lifestyle, it becomes truly inspirational.

In my opinion, a healthy lifestyle must include a deeper purpose to be fully transformative because it improves your mental health. Health is a complex topic but having purpose is what truly completes our lives. Homesteading gives us that purpose.

The Initial Challenge of Homesteading

As I've said many times, homesteading is a simple lifestyle. But it's also hard work. The initial challenges catch an unprepared person completely off-guard. Waking up early to milk Betty the Cow is quite tedious at first. Manual labor hits hard at first. The challenges of securing a property, planting your first crops, buying your first animal, and developing the vitality necessary for hours of manual labor are all stressful. But unlike the hustle of city life, it's not unending stress. There is light at the end of the tunnel!

With that said, let's address a common misconception of homesteading. We know it's dirty work so a lot of people tend to believe that it has other detrimental effects on our health. After all, if you are shoveling manure all day, wouldn't you be exposing yourself to a ton of unhealthy germs?

The answer is yes but it isn't quite as bad as many people believe. In fact, it's actually healthier. To explain why, let's look at the Hygiene Hypothesis as posted by the FDA.[iv]

According to the Hygiene Hypothesis, people who live in extremely clean environments are more susceptible to infections. Their immune system isn't being exposed to enough germs to educate the immune system to learn and develop antibodies to adapt.

In short, the immune system is weaker because it's sitting on the couch all day eating Cheetos!

So initially, working on a homestead will trigger allergies and force your immune system to get off the couch and work. This leads to fatigue and some side effects that will make it seem unhealthy at first. But once your immune system adapts, you'll be healthier than ever!

Start the Journey to a Healthier Life

There's no reason to wait until you've invested in a homestead to start living a healthier life. If health is your motivation, then make the decision to be healthy right now. Don't wait until tomorrow. Don't wait until tonight. Commit to a healthier lifestyle right this very minute!

The fact is that you don't need to be on a homestead to eat healthier and exercise. All it takes is a commitment. A commitment to your health, and the health of your family.

Start by donating all of your processed, unhealthy foods to a food shelter. Get them out of your kitchen and start filling it with the same types of foods you'll have on your homestead. You don't have to spend thousands on "organic" foods though. Just transition to whole foods. They won't be as healthy as those you'll grow yourself, but this is a good starting point.

Exercise every day. Even taking a short walk every morning will do wonders for your health. You don't want to wait until you're working on the homestead to start exercising. Trust me! You'll regret it if you wait! There's no need to drop a lot of money on a gym membership though. In fact, you should opt to save that money toward buying your homestead! Just find activities that keep you physically active. Don't spent your whole day off staring at a television. Get out of the house and do something. Hiking and biking are great starts, and don't involve spending the money you're trying to save.

Finally, consider growing a few crops where you currently live. The next chapter will go into detail about this topic, so I'll save the details for later. What I want to emphasize is that growing your own produce is the core of homesteading, so you need to take a few baby steps right now. You'll make mistakes when you first start gardening. It's better to make them on a small garden than it is to make them while growing an acre of crops!

Reason #4: Going Green

One of the biggest draws to homesteading is that it's seen as an eco-friendly lifestyle. A lot of people choose this life because they dream of living "off-the-grid." This long-term goal serves as great motivation to start a homestead but isn't quite as straight-forward as many tend to believe.

As I've said many times, homesteading is about building a self-sufficient lifestyle. This leads to reduced expenses and lowers our carbon footprint. So going green not only helps the environment. It helps our bank account too!

There are certain drawbacks that prevent complete off-the-grid living and we'll discuss those in a moment. But even the act of creating an eco-friendly homestead isn't quite as straight-forward as many tend to believe. Let's start by looking at the exact nature of going green.

In general, going green simply means that we take steps to reduce the damage we're doing to the environment. Every decision we make asks the important question, "How harmful is this to the environment?"

There are a lot of considerations that homesteaders must make. Some are easy choices while others will require time, creativity, or a combination of the two. Here are a few examples:

- Use organic pest control rather than toxic commercialized products. This is not only healthier for the environment, but healthier for your family.
- Use organic fertilizers. Commercialized fertilizers create chemical runoff that pollutes drinking water.
- Reduce fossil fuels. Technology advancements has made this much easier to achieve. Solar panels and automotive EV technology have advanced quite a bit in the past decade, and it doesn't look to be slowing down.
- Using 100% natural animal feed. Many commercial feed brands come loaded with antibiotics, steroids, and other unnatural ingredients.
- Raising your own food rather than relying on industrialized farms.
- Making your own clothes is a great way to reduce industrialized waste and is a great family activity.

The list goes on and on but I'm sure you get the point. Going green doesn't just benefit the entire planet. It makes life so much simpler. It also takes quite a bit of planning to achieve.

Going Green Challenges Everything You've Learned

Mindset is the greatest challenge you'll have to overcome if you want to live an eco-friendly lifestyle. Living green challenges everything you've learned so developing the right mindset keeps you anchored when things seem tough.

First of all, the challenge of setting up renewable systems is the first and perhaps most intimidating obstacle you'll face. Although it saves a ton of money in the long-term, the initial costs are quite high. It's easier if you plan it into the initial stages of starting your homestead though.

For instance, when having your well dug, have a hand pump installed along with the motor. If you have to repair the roof of the home before moving in, look into the cost of installing solar panels. Chances are that it will be more affordable to combine it with the repairs.

When setting up your farm, install a rain gathering system that catches and stores rainwater for irrigation.

Those are just three examples out of hundreds of small things you can do to meet the challenges of setting up a green homestead. It's much easier to tackle this stuff now than it would be to deal with it once you've gotten into the groove.

Of course, that's not always possible so you can also choose a single item to change so that it stays manageable.

The biggest challenges with adding renewable resources to your homestead are hidden legal requirements. Do your homework on the legal requirements of the location where you will be planting roots. For instance, you can't just install solar panels without a permit. There are also requirements as to how you keep animals and their living conditions. Going against the rules may result in fines and other legal trouble.

Another essential factor to keep in mind is that you need to have backup options when using eco-friendly systems. If you live in an area with extremely cold winters, be sure that you have a form of backup heat to use just in case you happen to run out of wood. I know this seems unlikely, but it's always better to be safe than sorry when it comes to the health and safety of your family.

Living completely off-the-grid is not always possible since you need permits to do just about anything in most locations. This is true even if you live miles from anyone else. Of course, there are exceptions. Part of the challenge is finding out what's possible and what's not depending on where you are planning to homestead.

Go Green Starting Today

Why wait until you are living at your homestead to start developing the required habits for living a greener life? Start today and make the transition to homesteading much easier. Making certain small changes right now lessens the stress of the transition to the homesteading lifestyle. Plus, you need to make sure you'll be comfortable with the lifestyle required for homesteading.

Five simple tips for going green:

1. Start with small things. Rather than turning on all the lights in the house to perform various tasks during the day, open the curtains and use natural light. Turning on the lights during the day for common tasks is a bad habit that we've carried our whole lives and it's one of the easiest to change.

2. Another easy change is to shop at local farmer's markets rather than visiting the produce section at the supermarket. Industrialized agriculture leaves a huge carbon footprint so by supporting local farmers, you are lessening the damage. Plus, it gets you into the habit of eating fresher foods. You can also look into a local community supported agriculture (CSA) program. Even big cities like New York have them. For more information check out https://www.localharvest.org.

3. Start drying your laundry outside by hanging it on a clothesline. This saves a ton of money on electricity.

4. Collect rainwater for watering your household plants. Check the legality of this in your local area before collecting rainwater though. Believe it or not, this is illegal in some communities. Also never leave rainwater sitting around outside. Collect it as soon as the rain has passed and store it in a sealed location. Rainwater attracts pests.

5. Set up a sewing station and learn how to make your own clothes. Start with small pillowcases and work your way to more complex weaving.

There are hundreds of small steps you can take so use this list as an example of potential energy saving ideas and grow that list over time until these changes become habitual. None of them are difficult. We just tend to pick up bad habits that we carry into adulthood but once you shift your mindset, you'll find yourself naturally choosing green over convenience.

Free Goodwill

Did you know that helping others can actually make you live longer, feel happier, and even earn more money? It's true, and I want you to experience these benefits for yourself. That's why I have a question for you: would you be willing to lend a hand to someone you've never met before, if it didn't cost you a dime and you didn't get any recognition for it?

If your answer is yes, then I have a small request for you. There are people out there who are just starting out on their homesteading journey, and they need your help. They're searching for information and guidance, and you can provide that by leaving an honest review of this book. Your review will help someone leave behind the stress and chaos of the rat race and build a simpler, more fulfilling life for themselves and their loved ones.

By taking a minute right now to share your thoughts on this book, you could make a huge difference in someone's life. People do, in fact, judge a book by its cover (and its reviews) By leaving one yourself, you could be the reason why someone decides to take the first step towards self-reliance and sustainability. So, if you have found this book valuable so far, please go ahead and leave that review now, and know that you're making a positive impact on people just like you who had to start their homesteading journey with that first step. It is my greatest desire for you, that you'll discover solutions here and on my website, TheGreenHomesteader.com, that will improve your own path to self-reliance!

PS- if you feel good about helping a fellow prospective homesteader, you are the kind of people I like to associate with, so I'm that much more excited to help you along the path to self-reliance and hope you love the bonus material I'm going to share with you in Chapter 11.

PPS- Life hack: if you introduce something valuable to someone, they associate the value with you. So, if you'd like to receive goodwill directly from another beginning homesteader – send this book their way.

Thank you from the bottom of my heart. Now that you've left your review, let's get back to the book and find out what it costs to get started on the path to self-reliance.

-Your devoted supporter, Elise

Chapter 7

Can I Make Money From Homesteading?

So now it's time to address a common question with homesteading – should you expect to make money from your homestead? It's not impossible. Many homesteaders get to the point where they are able to earn a full-time income from their homestead. However, this takes a lot of time and patience. So, my advice is to go into this with the mindset that you won't be able to earn a full-time income with homesteading. At least, not initially.

Most people who start out on their homesteading journey discover that they need multiple income streams. That's okay because it forces a more creative mindset so don't let it discourage you.

In fact, it's a good idea to have multiple streams of income anyway. Nothing is guaranteed. One crop could fail, or you could lose dozens of livestock from some new disease. Never put all of your eggs in one basket because all it takes is one ill-timed stumble to break everything.

Did you know that successful, financially secure homesteaders have multiple streams of income? Some of them even earn six figures from their homestead while also meeting all of their family's needs. In short, they would be completely fine if society was to fail but they also get to enjoy modern living now. That's the ultimate homesteading goal.

Monetizing Your Homestead Requires a Touch of Creativity

Businesses learn to monetize as many of their normal processes as possible to squeeze every penny out of them. This same mindset is used to monetize a homestead. Take a close look at anything you're doing and ask yourself the important question: Is there a way I can earn extra money from this without disrupting the process?

Some homesteading income models are obvious while others take some creativity. There are a lot of income streams that most homesteaders never even consider. The ones who do are living their dream life!

We're going to look at some ideas that you can use on your homestead to generate income. The goal is to slowly add income until eventually your homestead stands on its own.

Capitalize On Your Gardening Efforts

Produce is the first money-making homesteading venture that comes to mind. It's understandable since fresh local produce is so popular. But how much can you really earn from selling locally? It's not going to be enough to sustain your whole family. So, you need to think outside of the box a bit.

First of all, you need to make sure you save enough produce for your family's needs before selling it. Otherwise, what's the point of homesteading in the first place?

Once you set aside enough for your needs, you'll find that your income will be quite limited. You should always sell extra but there are other ways you can get the most from limited resources.

Keep all of the seeds. When you harvest healthy plants, they will produce a lot of seeds. If you started with heirloom varieties, these seeds can be sold as heirloom seeds. In other words, people are willing to invest in heirloom seeds because they take on the traits from previous generations and provide a consistent crop year after year. Unlike genetically modified, or specialized varieties whose seeds either don't germinate or produce Frankenstein varieties. Not only are heirloom varieties more resilient to changes in the climate, but they also produce consistent vegetables that taste better and have more flavor. They are a hot commodity that can generate income and there's no way you'll use them all. So why waste them?

To sell heirloom seeds, collect and dry them after harvest. Maybe have some information about their breed or have pictures that show the healthy crops they come from. You can even sell them alongside a few vegetables that produced them.

Another strategy is to grow herbs throughout your crops. Certain herbs serve as natural pest repellants so you can space them strategically throughout vegetables. Then during harvest, dry those herbs and sell the majority of them. Herbs like basil, thyme, and parsley are always in high demand.

Finally, you can turn to canning, dehydrating, or freeze drying to preserve some of your crop yield. These preserved vegetables will sell for a higher income than the fresh produce. Plus, food preservation is a fun family activity. Get creative! You can use extra produce to make jellies, soups, and sauces that can be sold at farmer's market.

Raising Farm Animals to Generate Income

The other go-to homesteading venture is to raise animals. There are a lot of income opportunities, many of which are not commonly thought of. Let's start with the most common – chickens.

A chicken coop will be one of the first items you build on your homestead. Eggs are highly valuable because they provide a ton of nutrients and tending to laying hens isn't extremely demanding work. It can be dirty if not done right, but it won't eat away an entire day.

Start by planning on having enough chickens so that you're egg yield is higher than your family's requirement. There are lots of online resources that provide estimated egg yields by poultry variety to get you started. Sell any extra eggs or use them for things like homemade mayonnaise. You'd be surprised at the popularity of homemade mayonnaise. It's my son's favorite!

You can also raise some chickens for meat, but this is more labor intensive and requires more land. Do your research before starting down this path.

A much better option is to raise pullets. Pullets are chickens who have reached 6 weeks of age. This is the point at which their care becomes easier, and they are less likely to die from improper heat control, overcrowding, or lack of hydration. Baby chicks have a mortality rate of 1-5 percent and failure to thrive is every breeder's bane. As for me, I keep one rooster and let the hens do all the work. It takes the guess work as well as the hard work out of the equation.

Another great use for animals is to produce dairy. Fresh milk has become a high demand product in rural areas, so this is a great way to earn some extra income. Of course, if your family consumes a lot of dairy products, then you might find yourself unable to produce enough milk to sell.

Finally, cultivating compost is another way to earn some extra income. With the high cost of commercial fertilization products as well as concerns about chemical shortages, more farmers will have to return to basics, and that starts with compost. Compost is the ultimate fertilizer, and it has to go somewhere so why waste it?

Chances are that you will have more than enough for your own use too so you might as well sell the excess.

Teach Skills for Extra Income

You learn a lot of valuable skills when starting a homestead so why not share those skills to help others? Here's the thing. People are willing to pay to learn new skills and there aren't a lot of homesteading tutors available. Yet, there are people who would love to learn how to can their own food or hone their gardening skills. I know because I recently attended a class on making Fire Cider. Not only did I learn something new, but I also made contacts with others who were interested in homesteading or purchasing locally grown products.

With your blossoming experience, it's possible to schedule one-on-one training in addition to hosting a weekly live workshop. Just find a schedule that works best for you.

You can even mix some of your daily homesteading activities into the workshop to show learners how to perform specific tasks. I'm not saying that you have them do the work but let them watch while you explain what's happening.

It's also possible to create an online learning program that teaches important homesteading skills. You would need to have someone film you as you carry out everyday activities and then provide a voice over explaining it. But this type of content is in high demand and there's not a lot of competition.

Finally, if you are homeschooling your own kids, then you might be able to offer these homeschooling lessons to other families for a small fee. You're already putting in the work to create the lessons anyway so it's not going to require any extra work.

Offer Homesteading Experiences on Airbnb

Vacation experiences are in high demand right now. I've read countless stories about everyday people making a ton of money by transforming their extra bedroom, guest house, or sometimes even a camping spot into an experience. For those of you who are not familiar with Airbnb, this online service allows people to book their extra rooms to visitors. It works like a hotel in that the individual rents the room for a set number of days.

What people have discovered is that they can offer much more than just a boring room by creating a theme or experience. Your homestead is a great experience waiting to happen. You just have to highlight the benefits.

Welcome travelers to a rural atmosphere where they can see live animals and camp under the stars. List a guest room or simply add a convenient camping site to an unused section of your property. If it has a view or access to a water feature, even better. You can also include a tour of your homestead or some local sites to add to the experience.

Just keep in mind that people use Airbnb for the experience, not just a place to sleep so you need to put some thought into what kind of experience you can offer.

Farm Sitting for Extra Income

If your homestead is still maturing and you find yourself with free time, consider becoming a farm sitter to earn some extra income. Ask around your neighborhood to see if anyone needs occasional farm sitting. This will get you some experience and gets people talking about you. Then you can expand your services if you want.

Just don't let farm sitting take the place of developing your own homestead. The end goal should always be growing and developing your own self-sufficient lifestyle. But looking after someone's farm while they go on vacation isn't likely to compromise your own progress. Plus, it will earn you some much-needed income as well as providing experience.

Don't let it become overwhelming though. The last thing you want is for a side venture to create stress in your life. I recommend you keep a calendar and schedule your time using a priority system. Always schedule your own homesteading activities first.

Raising Bees

Bees add tremendous value to your homestead and they're actually not as difficult to keep as many tend to believe. Let's start with the benefits of beekeeping for a homestead.

Bees serve as pollinators so your crops will thrive in their presence. Due to their importance, equipment is easy to find and not even that expensive. You can buy a complete colony with a queen to get started. So, it's never been easier to start raising bees than it is right now.

Gardens become more colorful due to their symbiotic relationship with bees. Without getting into the science behind it, one of the side effects of pollination is that it leverages our garden and helps all of our plants thrive. It's not unusual for certain fruit crops to experience a 50% increase in harvest. Bees essentially help plants to reproduce, which leads to more fruits. The same is true for certain vegetables too.

You monetize bees by collecting honey and then selling it at the farmer's market. People absolutely love fresh honey, so you'll find yourself selling out very quickly.

However, bees are a long-term investment, so you won't be able to start gathering honey until their second year. If you don't leave their stockpile of honey for their first winter, the bees will not survive so it's important that you don't mess with their food reserves right away.

Once they are past their first winter, bees will start to deliver gallons of honey. In fact, it's not unheard of for a single hive to produce over 30 pounds of honey!

Furthermore, beeswax is also a way to earn some income from bees. And if that's not enough, you can earn money by selling the bees themselves.

While beekeeping isn't going to make you rich by itself, it boosts the efficiency of certain plants and benefits your homestead.

Chapter 8

What Does it Cost to Get Started?

Finances are what cause most people's homesteading dreams to come crashing down to reality. I won't lie. It takes a considerable investment to create a homestead that will provide enough for your whole family to become self-sufficient if you don't already own property. But it's also not as daunting as it might seem right now.

The key is to break it all down into manageable steps and build up to a life of self-sufficiency. You won't reach that point overnight. It takes dedication, sacrifice, and hard work to build a self-sufficient lifestyle.

Know Your Family's Needs

Homesteading costs are directly tied to your family's individual needs. There's no "one size fits all" financial strategy for starting a homestead. So, the first thing you have to do is identify your unique needs. By this point, you have identified your goals so you have a better picture of what the end game will look like.

Now look at your current living situation and answer some important questions.

- Do you rent or own your property?
- Do you have land that can be used right now for gardening or raising animals?
- If so, how much land is available?
- If you live in an apartment, are you willing to move to a rental or buy a small home for farming?
- How much debt do you have right now?
- How many people are you supporting?
- How many of the people you are supporting are able to help with daily chores?

These are all basic questions that must be addressed. Your living situation right now is your starting point. So, you have your starting point and the ending point of your homesteading journey. You just have to determine the steps required to get from A to Z.

Costs Associated with Homesteading

As I said earlier in this book, it's nearly impossible to break away from society completely so you will still have expenses that you have to keep up with. You may have to buy a property, invest in equipment, and need to continue saving for emergencies. The bottom line is we live in a society governed by money, so unless you are able to go completely off-grid and barter for commodities like salt and toilet paper, you are going to continue needing at least some form of income.

Of course, you can minimize costs to a point by creating a self-sufficient lifestyle, but you can't eliminate it completely. Even if you live completely off-the-grid, you'll still have to pay taxes or Uncle Sam will come knocking on your door and take your property away from you.

Keep in mind that you should never put your finances under stress by going into a ton of debt to start homesteading. Start slow and do it the right way. Homesteading is hard enough without the added burden of financial hardships topping it off. This is a gradual process.

So, let's dive into the costs associated with owning a homestead. I'll stick to the common costs that are incurred by all homesteads, but depending upon your unique situation, your costs could vary.

Property Purchase

You'll need land in order to build your new homesteading life. This is the biggest investment you'll have to make. There's really no getting around spending money here. Even if you get a property as inheritance or come into it some other way, you'll still have to pay property taxes.

Food

Many beginners go into homesteading under the impression that they will grow everything they eat. But that's not really feasible unless you own a large property and are coming into it as a master gardener. Chances are that you'll need to buy at least some of the food for your family. Bread, sugar, baking soda, and salt are all examples of things you'll probably buy. With that said, homesteading will cut your grocery bill to a fraction of what it is without homesteading.

Utilities

Unless you want to live completely off-the-grid, you'll have to pay for utilities like electricity, internet, and a phone. Installing solar panels and using other forms of renewable energy is a great long-term goal but chances are that you won't be able to have this stuff immediately. So go ahead and plan for utilities and continue to set aside funds for the projects that will help reduce your long-term utility costs.

Maintenance Costs

Repairing fences, chicken coops, and even making repairs to your home are all going to cost money. Sure, you can do this yourself and you'll feel great when you learn the skills to do so. But materials still cost money and there are some tasks like electrical work where you are better off bringing in a professional, unless of course you are a licensed electrician. Besides, your time is best spent tending to crops and animals if they will be providing income for your family.

Medical Costs

I don't recommend you stop visiting the dentist or getting regular checkups. That would just be irresponsible. Plus, your animals also deserve love and care. So be prepared to pay for these expenses. Don't bank on a doctor or veterinarian who earns a six-figure income to be willing to barter for their services.

Initial Startup Costs

You have to buy animals to start your farm. Fences have to be built. You need farm equipment, and tools. There are a lot of costs on the front end of a homestead that you simply can't get around. Also don't skimp on quality here. Once you've made this initial investment, you'll be able to breed future generations of animals and get seeds to sow your next crops. But the first time, it's going to cost you.

Animal Feed

Animal feed is also a cost that many beginners don't consider, as wild as that might sound. Maybe they think they'll just feed them scraps? Unfortunately, it doesn't work like that. If you want healthy animals, then you need high quality feed. Always choose fully organic feed if it fits into your budget so that you're not pumping your animals full of additives that will impact their health in the long-term. It costs more but your animals will be healthier and happier. And remember, even animals that free-range and graze may need supplemental feed, so don't count on your free-range chickens making it through the winter without supplemental feed.

Starting a Homestead with Little to No Money

If you are planning to start a homestead and you have limited funds, the key is to take gradual steps toward a long-term goal. As we've seen throughout this book, you can develop a homesteading mentality and start developing solid habits right now no matter what your current living situation is. So even if you don't have the money to invest in a property right away, you can start saving and prepping. This is part of the homesteading journey.

There are numerous success stories of people who have created a self-sufficient lifestyle without having a large bank account. Sure, it's hard work and requires a lot of discipline and dedication, but that just makes the payoff much more fulfilling.

Start saving money right now. When you develop a habit that lowers your expenses, start putting that money into a savings account. The key phrase throughout this section is to "save money."

Create a Budget Right Now!

The first step to saving money is to learn the proper budgeting skills. You need to learn to live off less money than you currently earn. That's the only way to save money. Fortunately, most people find that once they break their expenses down to the bare minimum, they can actually survive on just half of their income.

Find opportunities to cut unnecessary expenses. Here are some examples:

- Lower your grocery bill by growing your own vegetables.
- Stop making unnecessary purchases. Only buy things you absolutely need.
- Consider selling things you no longer use.
- Pay off debt. Interest rates will eat away at a budget so by paying off debt, you eliminate these interest payments.
- Cut all unnecessary expenses like cable.
- Buy in bulk. Products that have long-term use should always be purchased in bulk. It saves quite a bit of money in the long-term.

Finally, add extra income in your budget to a savings account so that you can invest it later.

To get you started you can download our budget planner and goal-setting workbook from the Green Homesteader website. https://www.TheGreenHomesteader.com.

Prepare for Tax Laws Associated with Homesteading

Now it's time to take a close look at one of the most tedious aspects of homesteading. No matter how much we try and break away from modern life, taxes are the one thing that we can't escape. Taxes will catch the unprepared homesteader off-guard and can completely derail all of those plans for self-sufficiency.

My job is to make sure you're prepared for this new lifestyle so you are not caught off-guard. The first important tax lesson is that your taxes will vary by state. There are certain generalized tips I will provide but for the exact details, you'll need to check with your local tax agency.

With that said, let's start by reviewing a few of the general tips that will help you get a grasp on the taxes associated with homesteading.

First and foremost, you have to determine whether your homesteading activities count under the IRS definition of farming. The IRS defines a farmer as an entity that "cultivates, operates, or manages a farm for profit."[v]

Most homesteaders miss the "for profit" part. If your homestead activities are producing foods that are being stored for your family and not sold, then you likely won't qualify for the tax exemptions given to farmers. This activity would be defined as a hobby.

However, if you are selling produce and earning all of your income through the farm, then you would qualify as a farmer in the eyes of the IRS.

On the other hand, if you are working another job to support your homestead's finances, you should check with your accountant. Some of your expenses may be deductible. Just because you are working your land for profit doesn't mean you will make a profit. Many farmers operate at a loss, especially during the early years. I planted a thousand trees in 2021 that won't produce until 2026 or later. The costs associated with maintaining my orchard until it produces a profit are all deductible.

In addition to the IRS, your local state and county often have tax breaks for farming activities such as discounted property taxes. Definitely talk to your accountant and local tax assessor to find out what the rules are in your state. My property taxes went from nearly $2,500 year to $486 per year because I own more than 15 acres and planted a 5-acre orchard.

Here's the tricky part though. Regardless of how the IRS sees you, if you sell any produce from your homestead, then it must be reported as income, so you'd better brush up on your book-keeping skills. There are also other types of income that most people don't consider which might impact you as well. Bartering and cancelled debt are generally defined as reportable income. Since this varies locally, you should check your local tax regulations for exact details.

Part II of Schedule F[vi] will provide details on the expenses allowed for homesteaders.

Understanding Deductions

Certain tax deductions apply to everyone while others are reserved for individuals whom the IRS deems as "farmers." Again, check all of the regulations in your local area for more exact details. That's the common theme of this section. This can be quite confusing. Sometimes my head spins just thinking about it so I'm going to lay it out in the simplest way possible.

Don't fall prey to the many misconceptions that plague so many new homesteaders. Not every expense can be deducted from your taxes. For instance, home repairs that do not directly affect the production value of the homestead cannot be deducted. However, if you have a barn that incurs damage, then you might be able to deduct it depending on whether or not the IRS sees it as a hobby or a profession.

In short, if an expense doesn't directly affect income generated by the homestead, then it cannot be deducted. With that in mind, here are some examples of potential deductions to keep in mind:

- Farm equipment

- Seeds
- Fertilizer
- Depreciation
- Feed
- Farm Insurance
- Loan Interest for Farm Related Debt
- Storage Costs

These are the most common deductibles for your homestead but let's look at a few that many people don't even consider.

Some individuals are able to deduct part of their utilities and other home costs from their taxes. If you use your home for tasks that directly tie to income generated by your homestead, then you might qualify. For instance, families with equipment in their basement that's used to can food for sale would be able to deduct a certain percentage of their utilities. IRS publication 225[vii] explains this in more detail.

The biggest tax benefit that farmers receive is the ability to deduct net operating costs from their taxes. However, only homesteaders who qualify as a "farmer" are able to do this. This tax law takes into account the unpredictability of farming.

Let's say that you are a homesteader who grows enough crops to feed your family and sells the rest on the market to generate income to pay other expenses. If you experience a significant drop in crop yield that causes your farm profits to result in a loss compared to all income from the previous year, then that loss can be used as a deduction.

In fact, you might be able to carry this loss of income back several years and deduct it to receive a partial refund from previous taxes paid. This loss can also be carried forward several years to help mitigate the risks of future problems.

This is a complex process, so you'll need a tax expert to fill out the proper filing paperwork. The problem is that a lot of homesteaders don't even know about this deduction, so they never pursue it.

Homestead Exemption

Homestead exemption is a salvation for the most difficult times in your life. Think of it like a safety net that protects your home from major, catastrophic life events. Having just gone through an unprecedented pandemic, I'm sure we can all agree that mitigating against these types of events will help us sleep better at night.

Even though homesteading is about becoming self-sufficient, it takes time to reach that level. In the meantime, your home will be vulnerable to economic instability, so you have to go into this new lifestyle with the understanding that you live in a governed country, so we're all subject to its laws.

Homestead exemption is put in place to protect homeowners from creditors. It keeps them from being able to force a sale of your home to clear certain debt. Furthermore, you can use it to lower your property taxes so it's essential that you understand the basics of homestead exemption.

In this context, the word "homestead" means "primary residence." Homestead exemption only applies to a primary residence, which is an important distinction. Homeowners must apply for this exemption so be sure you actually follow through with this step. This is done at the local level so I can't give you an exact process. Visit your county tax office to learn more.

How Does Homestead Exemption Work?

There are actually two ways that homestead exemption is enforced. Homestead exemption in general is a shield that protects against unforeseen circumstances like the death of a spouse, bankruptcy, and other factors that lead to financial instability.

On the other hand, we have homestead tax exemption which lowers the amount of property taxes paid on a primary residence. This also protects against property tax raises by setting a maximum amount that taxes on primary residences can be raised in a given year.

For either method to be enforced, the residence must be a primary living space. The exact nature of enforcement is different depending on the state, but I will go over a few examples, so you get an idea of how it works. Just keep in mind that this information might not apply to you. They are just examples.

The first thing worth mentioning is that certain states set a limit on the value of a home that can qualify for homestead exemption. This is designed to keep rich people from finding ways to bypass taxes. However, the problem is that homestead properties can also be quite expensive depending on its size and how much you develop it. Keep this in mind before purchasing and/or expanding on your property.

Most states issue homestead exemptions using one of two methods:

- Amount is based on a percentage of the property's value.
- Amount is a set value.

Exemptions based on a percentage of the property's value is going to be the biggest benefit to most homesteaders since this exemption will rise as your property becomes more valuable. For example, a $200,000 property owner in an area with 1% taxes would have to pay $2,000 in taxes each year.

Now let's assume you live in an area that provides a set $50,000 in relief. You deduct that amount from the property's value so you would only have to pay taxes on $150,000, which comes to $1,500. Of course, using that same scenario, if your property happens to be valued at $50,000 or less, then you wouldn't have to pay anything at all.

Research homestead exemption laws in an area before buying a property. Choosing a location with the right tax laws will make a huge difference.

Local Agricultural Tax Breaks

In addition to property and income tax breaks, you may also be able to claim local agricultural tax breaks. In my state, Tennessee, I am able to get a sales tax exemption on agricultural products related to my farming activities. That means I don't pay sales tax on things like animal feed, fertilizer, seed stock, animals, agricultural diesel, tractors and other farming equipment, and the list goes on. This is definitely worth looking into before you decide to buy a property.

Local Farming Programs

If the above reasons weren't enough benefit to motivate you, you'll be excited to hear that many states have local farming programs. In my state, I can get up to a 50% refund on things like cross-fencing and building animal enclosures. Your local extension office has a plethora of information, so reach out to them about special programs and grant opportunities.

Grant Opportunities

And speaking of grant opportunities, there are several programs available to farmers for a variety of reasons. I recently applied and was awarded a grant to put in an irrigation system for my orchard. Check out Grants.gov or contact your local extension office since they tend to administer many of them.

Veterans Benefits

While this may not apply to everyone, some areas have special benefits or discounts for Veterans that can add up over time. A good example is Oregon, Veterans who live in Oregon can get lifetime license plates, meaning they don't have to apply for new tags every year.

There are also programs for low-income veterans interested in farming. Check out the USDA website for details about some of their latest programs for beginning farmers.

The Farmer Veteran Coalition also has grant programs, training and other resources that may be of interest.

Part 3

Make Sure You're Committed

Chapter 9

The Beginner's Garden

Transitioning to the homesteading way of life is a significant lifestyle change for many people so it's important that you make sure that it's the life you want. The previous chapter explored the major challenges that you'll face when starting a homestead. Now we'll look into some other small steps you can take right now in order to transition into the homesteading lifestyle.

Small is the keyword in that last statement. Homesteading isn't a life that you need to dive headlong into and then pick up the pieces as you go. Those who take that approach often find themselves overwhelmed and spend their days carrying a lot of stress. They start to regret their decision. Their homestead suffers and their dream of a self-sufficient lifestyle quickly turns into a nightmare.

By starting small, you achieve two important things. The first is that you prepare yourself mentally and physically for the transition. Secondly, you are ensuring that homesteading is truly the lifestyle you want to live. It's one thing to dream of self-sufficiency but it's quite another to actually start living that life.

Dreams often paint a much different picture than reality. By taking small steps now, you are testing whether homesteading is truly the life for you and your family. So before turning your world upside-down, test the homesteading waters with some small, yet pivotal changes to your lifestyle.

Now the only thing to decide is where to start. There are a lot of possibilities so I'll go over a few amazing hobbies that can serve as a steppingstone to deciding whether or not homesteading is right for you.

Starting a Small Garden

Test out your green thumb by learning the basics of gardening. What makes this such an amazing first step is that you can start growing no matter where you live. Of course, you'll be limited by space and climate, but you can at least get your hands dirty a bit and learn how certain plants react to certain conditions.

Let's look at a few tips that you'll need to know before you start growing your own food and herbs.

How to Choose the Right Beds

At this point, you are probably still trying to make the final decision on whether or not you are truly committed to homesteading. So, if you're working with limited space where you need to get creative, using flower bedding kits is a great alternative. These kits range anywhere from aluminum corner kits with some building required to full blown beds that are easily placed in the yard.

I won't go into specific details about individual beds since there are so many. You can easily search on Google to find something that fits your yard. Rather than look at individual designs and brands, I'll go over a few factors to keep in mind when making your decision.

Where Will you Set up the Gardening Bed?

Most plants will need to get eight hours of direct sunlight each day so choose a location in your yard that is guaranteed to get enough sun. It's okay for plants to have more than eight hours but they will typically struggle if they receive less than eight hours.

Additionally, avoid areas that get saturated with water. The beds need a location where the soil can properly drain. Water buildup will lead to significant problems including things like root rot and attracting pests.

Good soil is another concern, so you're better off investing in a raised bed so you can put in your own soil blend. It's almost always going to be superior to what's naturally in your yard. This ensures proper drainage and gives you more control over the nutrients in the soil. I garden almost exclusively in raised beds because the soil quality is so superior, and the maintenance is almost nil.

You should first remove all of the grass and weeds from the area where you plan to install the gardening bed. You will also want to till the soil under the bed before installing it so that water is allowed to drain into the ground. Plus, the loose soil gives plants more room to take root. I also put down landscape fabric since most vegetables don't need more than 4-6 inches of soil if you create your own soil rather than using the native soil.

Once you have finally installed the bed, it's time to add soil. The exact soil mixture depends on the vegetables you plan to grow. If you're unsure, then you can use the standard 60/30/10 ratio:

- 60% Topsoil (store-bought)
- 30% Compost
- 10% Potting Soil

Although, I prefer to use Mel's Mix®. Mel's Mix® is a proprietary description based on the name of the guy who wrote the Square Foot Gardening books. It is a mixture of diatomaceous earth, peat moss, and compost. It's a bit costlier to create than the standard mix above, but my results have been phenomenal, so I stick with it. Besides, once you get your compost heap started, you won't have to buy expensive compost to add to the mix. I used to get so much chicken coop waste that my compost pile was growing at an exponential rate. That's changed since I moved to the deep bedding method, but you can find out more about that on our website https://www.TheGreenHomesteader.com since it is beyond the scope of this book.

Deciding What to Plant

The first rule is to choose vegetables that you and your family love to eat. Don't make the mistake of planting foods you and your family don't like. You'll end up being extremely frustrated if all your hard work goes to feed the neighbors or worse, goes to waste.

So, if you are a big salad eater, then lettuce and tomatoes are great starting crops. I'll list several great starting crops in the next section to help you make this decision.

The key is to learn to maximize your space without overcrowding your garden. Keep in mind that plants need a certain amount of space to breathe. Overcrowding a garden will place tremendous stress on the plants and they will never reach their full potential. On the other hand, spacing them too far apart isn't productive either since you're essentially wasting garden space and providing a fertile space for weeds to grow. I recommend you use a ruler or tape measurer to make sure you get the spacing right. I am a firm believer in Square Foot Gardening to maximize your space. Also consider going vertical. Did you know pumpkins can be grown on a trellis? You'd actually be amazed at how many plants you can grow vertically to save space.

Another thing to consider is how each plant grows and the impact it will have on neighboring plants. For instance, tomatoes might interfere with neighboring plants. To avoid this, you might need to construct a small cage around the tomato plants to keep the garden more manageable.

On the other hand, tomatoes would have little impact on a neighboring root vegetable like carrots. When working with limited space, this is an important decision.

Finally, consider starting with plants rather than seedlings. This will save up to a month on harvesting. Of course, this only works with small garden. The advantage is that it gives you faster access to the harvested vegetables.

Choose the Right Time to Plant

Okay so by now you've considered everything and have a gardening plan so all that's left now is to actually put roots into the ground. Choosing the right time to plant comes down to the type of vegetable you want to grow. Some plants are unable to tolerate colder temperatures, so these are only feasible to plant during early summer. On the other hand, crops like lettuce can be planted into late summer since they are resilient to cold temperatures.

The goal is to plan your garden so that you are growing something through spring, summer, and fall months. And don't let anyone tell you that you can't grow in any given season. I have friends who, by using a shade cloth grew vegetables in the Arizona summer, and others who by using cold frames grew lettuce and kale in the dead of a Wyoming winter. I'll give you some examples of what to plant later in this chapter along with the ideal times to plant them in moderate growing areas.

I highly recommend that you plan your garden using a calendar geared towards your specific USDA hardiness zone, so you know what to plant at specific times throughout the year. If you are unfamiliar with hardiness zones, check out https://planthardiness.ars.usda.gov for additional details.

Tips for Planting

Tending the soil just after planting is extremely important. For starters, the soil must be watered enough to make it moist throughout. Furthermore, it must remain moist throughout the entire germination process. This is so that the hardened exterior of the seed is softened enough for the sprout to break through it.

Any interruption in this process will force you to reseed the garden. Do not let the soil become dry. In fact, I highly recommend you cover the garden with garden fabric or a clear plastic covering (creates a greenhouse effect) during this period so that the sun is not able to directly impact the soil. This gives them time to establish roots so they can pull moisture from the soil.

Tips for Tending the Garden

Again, I cannot overstate how important the germination process is to your garden. This is a time when you'll need to check it two to three times per day to ensure the soil remains moist. Also, if any visitors decide to trespass and take root in your garden, then remove them immediately.

If you are gardening directly in the soil, rather than a prepared raised bed, you'll also need to apply fertilizer to the soil about once per month in order to ensure that your plants are getting the proper nutrients. Don't use chemical fertilizers though. Compost works wonders for gardens, and you need to get rid of those old leaves anyway! You can even save a few leftover eggshells to toss in the garden to replenish nutrients in the soil as well as provide additional aeration.

Plants need about one inch of rain per week to stay healthy. It's a good idea to install a rain gauge somewhere near the garden to keep track of how much natural water the plants have received. Of course, one inch is just a rule of thumb and won't be the case for all plants. But it's a good starting point for beginners.

You can check the soil's moisture by sticking your finger three to four inches in the ground where your plant is growing. If the soil is moist, then it doesn't need water. I recommend you do this every day, especially during the summer. If the soil is dry, then the plants need water.

Also keep in mind that plants might appear wilted during a hot summer day. This is a natural process that protects it from extreme sunlight. Checking the soil is how you tell whether or not the plants need water.

Finally, if your plants need water, then do so in the early morning or late afternoon. Water droplets will magnify the sun's light and damage the plants so by watering them in the early in the day or in the late afternoon, you're giving the water time to seep into the soil without sitting on the plant where they can become damaged by the heat of the sun or by remaining wet when the weather cools down. For best results, water the soil and not the green leafy parts of the vegetable.

Easiest Vegetables to Grow

There's something satisfying about growing your own food. Knowing that you grew it yourself gives you a sense of fulfillment. It's truly one of the best feelings in the world. One of the biggest benefits of gardening is that it inspires you to take an interest in the origin of the food going on your table. People who grow their own food tend to savor it more because they know what was required to put it on the table in addition to the fact that it just tastes better. Allowing the vegetables to ripen on the vine allows them to develop their full flavors. You'll be amazed at how much fulfillment even a small garden gives you.

But more importantly, trying your hand at starting a small garden will prove that you're truly dedicated enough to transition to a homesteading lifestyle. Just remember that the amount of work you'll have to do with your small garden is only a fraction of what will be required on a homestead when you plant a garden large enough to feed your family, so definitely consider raised beds if you have that option. Not only can you grow more food in less space, but there is also less maintenance involved.

Next, let's look at some of the best vegetables to grow to test out your new green thumb. Even if you're totally new to gardening, these vegetables are all undeniably beginner friendly.

Lettuce

At a Glance

Ideal Time to Plant: Spring to Fall

Germination Time: 2 to 15 days

Time to Harvest: 11 Weeks

Spacing: 12 Inches

Lettuce is perhaps the easiest vegetable to grow so it's a great place to start for those of you who might be completely new to gardening. It's also the most affordable so even big mistakes won't be costly. It's the vegetable that I recommend you start with for those very reasons.

First and foremost, you need to decide what type of lettuce you want to grow. The most common are Romaine and Iceberg so you'll probably want to start there. What makes lettuce such a great entry point into gardening is that it's quite resilient. You'd have to go out of your way to completely ruin a lettuce crop. Plus, it can withstand cold temperatures. Just be sure not to let frost come into contact with it and you'll be fine.

Lettuce can be planted anytime between early spring and early fall. It's best to avoid trying to grow it in the dead of winter. If the temperature does drop to the point where frost is expected, you can simply cover the crops with a plastic sheet overnight and it will be able to survive. Like I said, it's highly resilient.

Once the lettuce seeds have germinated, be sure to go through and remove clustered plants that have taken root. Lettuce needs 12 inches of spacing between plants in order to thrive.

Spinach

At a Glance

Ideal Time to Plant: Spring to Fall

Germination Time: 1 to 3 Weeks

Time to Harvest: 6 to 7 Weeks

Spacing: 8 Inches

Spinach is another great garden crop for beginners since it's so easy to grow. It shares many of the same characteristics as lettuce. Once the seeds have taken hold, you need to go through and clear any clusters to allow 8 inches of spacing between spinach plants. This gives them room to thrive.

It's also resilient to cold weather and can survive temperatures as low as 15 degrees so you won't need to worry too much about temperature if you live in a warmer climate. Just avoid planting it in the dead of winter and you'll be okay.

The fact that is takes less than two months for spinach from sowing to harvest is another added benefit.

Summer Squash

At a Glance

Ideal Time to Plant: Late Spring to Early Summer

Germination Time: 1 to 2 weeks

Time to Harvest: 7 to 9 Weeks

Spacing: 12 to 36 inches (depending on how you plant them)

As the name implies, summer squash is best grown in the summer. Such a plot twist, I know! This is another crop that requires moderate care so it's great practice.

Squash is also a vine plant, so it's recommended that you provide plenty of room for their vines to run. Consider a trellis, although you can also let the vines run along the ground. If you choose the latter option, make absolutely sure that you check the plants at least twice a day and pick the produce as soon as it's ready to prevent insect infestation and rot.

You'll know squash is ready to harvest when it's yellow and easy to break away from the stem.

Another common variety of summer squash is zucchini. If you've ever grown it, you'll know it's quite prolific and left to its own devices can grow to gigantic proportions. In fact, the world record for the longest zucchini is 8 feet 3.3 inches. And the Vermont state record for heaviest zucchini is 115 lbs. Now that would make a lot of bread!

Cucumbers

At a Glance

Ideal Time to Plant: Late Spring to Early Summer

Germination Time: 1 to 2 weeks

Time to Harvest: 8 to 10 weeks (depends on the variety)

Spacing: 12 to 36 inches (depending on how you plant them)

Cucumbers are a wonderful addition to a home garden for two reasons. For starters, it gives you practice growing a moderately difficult crop. The other reason is that you can pickle them to keep homemade dill pickles on-hand at all times.

You can plant cucumbers directly into the ground or use seeds so starting them is not too difficult. However, they are a warm climate crop so you can only grow them during the late spring and summer months. In certain climates, it's okay to carry over into early fall but that's always risky and not recommended.

Cucumbers are also a vine plant, so you need to give them a solid place to grow. Remember that the vines must also support the full weight of the cucumbers as they grow. You don't want them falling to the ground when growing.

This plant is also an excellent choice for apartment dwellers who have to start indoors. Just invest in a bucket for each plant and place them in direct sunlight for at least eight hours per day.

Finally, cucumbers require fertilizer in order to thrive – once a month should suffice. Use natural fertilizers that contain no chemicals so that you're not exposing your food to toxins.

Green Beans

At a Glance

Ideal Time to Plant: Late Spring to Early Summer

Germination Time: 1 to 2 Weeks

Time to Harvest: 8 to 9 Weeks

Spacing: 6 to 18 Inches (depending on how you plant them)

Green beans are another easy crop to grow, but this is one that requires a lot of space. Therefore, you will need an outdoor garden for this vegetable. Balcony gardening won't work unless you are able to provide a large trellis.

You'll want to start by choosing the type of green bean to grow. There are so many variations that it's impossible to list them all. Just keep in mind that certain types of green beans (Half-Runners) require you to remove strings after harvesting them. This is actually a fun activity for the entire family! I remember lazy afternoons on my aunt's farm pulling the strings and plucking off the stems in order to prepare them for canning.

If you don't want the hassle, then bush beans are a great alternate choice. These beans don't require stringing. You just pull them off the bush and you're good to go! You bypass all of the tedious hassle that comes with other types of green beans.

With that said, low nitrogen in the soil is one issue that many beginners run into with green beans. If the plants start to turn yellow, then you need to add bone meal or blood meal to the soil around them to supply adequate nitrogen.

Green beans also attract pests. Rather than using pesticide and poisoning your food source, plant a few herbs in between crops to serve as a natural deterrent. You can also set up bug traps. Watch my website https://www.TheGreenHomesteader.com for a companion planting guide due in the spring of 2023.

Bell Peppers

At a Glance

Ideal Time to Plant: Late Spring to Early Summer

Germination Time: 1 to 4 Weeks

Time to Harvest: 9 to 11 Weeks

Spacing: 18 to 36 Inches Apart

Bell peppers are another beginner friendly vegetable, one very high in vitamin C, that I highly recommend. The biggest consideration with bell peppers is that they must be grown in a warm climate so don't try growing this one outside of summer. Since it takes up to 11 weeks to grow, the planting window isn't as big as with other vegetables.

As with other plants, it's important to perform regular maintenance and remove weeds and other clusters so they have room to thrive.

With that said, it's easy to tell when bell peppers are ripe enough to harvest. They are green, yellow, or red depending on what type you are growing. If you notice their color fading, then you've waited too long.

Carrots

At a Glance

Ideal Time to Plant: All Seasons Except Winter

Germination Time: 1 to 3 Weeks

Time to Harvest: 9 to 11 Weeks

Spacing: 3 Inches

Root vegetables like carrots are easy to grow but harvesting gets a little tricky since they are underground so you can't actually see the product before removing it. Fortunately, there's an easy method that farmers have used for centuries with root vegetables. But let's start at the beginning.

You can sow carrots directly into the ground or in a container so there's no reason why apartment dwellers can't grow them. The real trick to growing any root vegetable is to make sure no other plants crowd it. In other words, plant them far enough apart and make sure to weed out any stray plants that try to take root in the same garden.

Another thing that makes all root vegetables so easy to grow is their resilience to temperature changes. They can survive in hot or cold climates. In some areas, it's possible to grow them year-round. Of course, in cold northern climates, you should avoid trying to grow them in the dead of winter.

Now comes the slightly tricky part. You will know that your plants are ready to test when they become green and bushy. However, before ripping up every single plant in the garden, pull out two or three from random spots. If all of those are ripe for harvest, then it's safe to remove all of the carrots from the garden. If not, then wait a week or so and perform the test again.

Tomatoes

At a Glance

Ideal Time to Plant: Late Spring to Early Summer

Germination Time: 1 to 2 Weeks

Time to Harvest: 8 to 14 Weeks

Spacing: 18 to 36 Inches

Tomatoes are one of the most popular choices for those choosing to grow their own food. But it's also one of the trickier crops to grow. While it's easy in concept, tomatoes require vigilant care and specific growing conditions to thrive.

What makes it so great is that these plants will produce tomatoes for several weeks, making the payout exceptionally high for the effort involved. Plus, tomatoes are delicious!

Tomatoes can be grown in a garden or on a balcony for apartment dwellers who are looking to get their hands dirty. It's imperative that they are not exposed to frost. Plus, they need quite a bit of water too – more than most crops I've listed in this chapter.

They also need cages or trellises that will support the full weight of a tomato to ensure they don't drop to the ground. There are tons of options available, and your choice will be dependent upon whether you grow them in the ground, in a pot, or if you are more adventurous, a hanging basket.

Finally, you must fertilize tomatoes with bone or blood meal at least once a month to replace the nitrogen in the soil if you are not using a prepared soil or Mel's Mix®. If you notice the plants turning yellow, add fertilizer sooner because that's a sure sign of nitrogen deficiency.

Five Easy Herbs for Beginners to Grow

Herbs are another great way for beginners to learn some of the basics of homesteading before investing a lot of money into this lifestyle. Many of these herbs are much easier to grow than the vegetables we just reviewed. They are also perfect for apartment dwellers who are looking into the homesteading life since they can be grown in small beds indoors, on a narrow windowsill, or on the balcony.

Backyard gardens can also benefit from certain herbs because they act as natural pest repellants. Since they are so small, certain herbs can be strategically planted between vegetables and grown at the same time to keep pests from eating away at your precious vegetables.

Finally, there are two categories of herbs and homesteaders are advised to learn to grow both types. Some types of herbs are used as seasoning when cooking while others are used for medicinal purposes.

Basil

Basil grows extremely fast, and each plant will provide a half-cup worth of leaves every week. Another amazing thing about basil is that clipping it will cause it to grow even fuller. So, it gets you into the habit of daily maintenance because you have to clip and nurture the plant every day in order to get the most out of it.

Thyme

Thyme is a key ingredient in a wide range of dishes and is perhaps the most resilient plant you'll ever grow. It can be planted outdoors year-round or planted in pots and kept indoors. It's also a versatile herb that's used in many soups and salads. I have mine in a couple of pots outdoors on the porch rail. Not only does it provide ample thyme for cooking, but it's also smells great as you are walking up the steps.

Bay Leaf

Bay leaves are a great addition to any home since they serve as a natural air freshener that makes your home smell sweet and earthly. They do require compost to thrive but there's an easy solution here. Every month or so, just add a small bit of leftover food to the soil, mix it in, and you'll be good to go!

Mint

Mint is another outstanding addition to the home. It's by far the easiest plant to grow. Plus, it serves as a natural insect repellant and a household air freshener. Give your home a minty aroma by placing a couple of mint plants around your home. They require very little maintenance. Just be sure to water them and they will thrive. One thing important to note however, is that mint is invasive. If you plant it outdoors, put it in a pot. You can bury the pot to keep it contained, but unless you want it to take over your flower beds, or worse yet, your entire yard, place it in a planter.

Oregano

Oregano is a smart choice for gardens because it actually nurtures other types of plants. If you are growing outdoors, add in a few oregano plants between each row and the rest of the crops will thank you. Just be sure to trim it weekly. Just like with basil, oregano grows thicker when regularly groomed. If you have to grow indoors, then place oregano next to other types of plants so they get the benefits.

Medicinal Herbs

As discussed in chapter 3, medicinal herbs can be used to create tinctures, glycerin, balms, and poultices to treat a variety of medical ailments and injuries. While they are no substitute for serious medical conditions, you'll be happily surprised by the number of ailments you can treat safely at home with herbs picked right from your garden.

Calendula

Calendula serves as an amazing natural antiseptic, so this is a must-have herb for homesteaders. It blooms year-round too. Just be sure to harvest the blooms before they form seeds and then dry them for later use. Calendula can be grown indoors or outdoors due to its versatility and provides a lovely flower for arrangements.

Cilantro

Now we come to an herb that can be used for cooking and is a great medical herb to have on-hand. It's a great digestive aid and also acts as a detoxifier for the body. It's best to grow cilantro either indoors or in a cool garden with a lot of moisture. Add it to at least one dish a week in order to reap the benefits to the body.

Rosemary

Rosemary is one of the top stimulants in the herbal family. If you find yourself turning to unhealthy energy drinks for a boost, then you should consider growing rosemary instead. It's also a great alternative to that second cup of coffee. What makes rosemary such a wonderful choice is that you only need one plant to meet all of your needs. You can simply plant one in the middle of your garden.

Mullein

Mullein is useful for healing bronchial infections so it's a must-have for homesteaders. This plant needs plenty of room to grow though since it stands at nearly six feet. Still, it's a great indoor plant that will add aesthetical appeal to your home.

Lavender

Lavender has a sweet aroma so it's another great indoor plant. But the real magic comes from its oil. Lavender oil helps cure insomnia, lowers stress, and is used to treat a number of skin conditions. It's also easy to grow this plant too. It needs plenty of sunlight and prefers a warm environment. So, keep it out of freezing temperatures and it will thrive.

Chapter 10

Pickling and Canning

Pickling is one of the go-to homesteading methods of preserving crops so it's a good idea to get into practice right now. There are two main methods of pickling that we'll discuss: vinegar pickling and fermentation. Both have their uses depending on the crop being grown and the unique needs of your family.

Vinegar is the easiest method, so I recommend you start there. Pickling with vinegar is easy because you can just put the produce into a jar of vinegar and store it immediately. No other work is required, although I certainly recommend you try out a few pickling recipes so that the food isn't bland in taste.

While fermented pickles are amazing, the process itself is a bit trickier so you could potentially spoil crops. Fermentation also takes much more planning. The process involves putting the produce through a fermentation process where it produces acid naturally. This process takes time and patience, but it also comes with several health benefits such as antioxidant, anti-microbial, anti-fungal, anti-inflammatory properties.

Again, I recommend you stick with vinegar in the beginning and perhaps experiment with fermentation pickling with a single jar or two to gain some experience.

What Produce Can be Pickled?

Honestly, pretty much any food can be pickled but they all have different rules that must be followed. For instance, you can pickle eggs, but you have to store them in the refrigerator. Pickled eggs also only have a lifespan of approximately four months. On the other hand, cucumbers can be stored either in the refrigerator or on the shelf, making them a staple food.

So, let's look at some of the different foods that can be pickled to help you get started.

Dill Pickles

This is the most common pickling recipe in North America. Dill pickling involves storing the produce in vinegar and dill, and sometimes garlic depending on the recipe and produce. Cucumbers are the most common dill pickled food, but the fact is that you can use different foods. Eggs and beans are both good choices. It's a really easy food to make with little effort so if you find yourself with extra cucumbers, then dill pickles are a great go-to recipe.

Kosher Style

Kosher is a variation of dill pickling but is done entirely through fermentation. Garlic is always one of the ingredients used since it's such a staple of Eastern European foods, which is the origin of Kosher Style pickling. You simply suspend the veggies in a salt-water solution, add in the appropriate ingredients, and then let nature do its job.

Half-Sour Pickling

Half-sour pickling follows a similar process to Kosher Style but rather than letting the food pickle completely, you will only let it ferment for half of the time. That makes this sourer than other types of pickles. These are crispier and take less time than other forms of pickling, making it appealing to a lot of people.

Sweet Pickles

For sweet pickles, you guessed it, sugar is added to the solution in order to give the foods a sweeter flavor. This is another popular pickling method. These pickles are made by adding sugar and other spices to the vinegar.

Pickling Tips

First and foremost, always follow a pickling recipe to make sure that you're doing it right. Getting this wrong will not only ruin your valuable produce, but it also risks your health. Pickling recipes are proven and ensure that you end up with a tasty and safe product.

It's a bad idea to get creative with pickling recipes since ingredients can interact with each other in ways you might not have considered. With pickling, the ratio of salt to vinegar is extremely important. Adding more salt might affect the safety of your pickles.

Also be sure that you buy kosher or pickling salt. Table salt will cloud the water and cake together, leading to uneven flavoring. So, it's not dangerous but it will make the pickles taste and look strange.

Follow a proven canning procedure too. There are a lot of canning guides with varying opinions, but I recommend you stick with reputable sources such as the USDA. Again, this is to protect your health since the process can be quite tricky. I'm including a whole section on canning right after this one. Canning is tricky so it's important that you follow specific rules in order to guarantee the integrity of your food.

Another important tip is to only use commercially produced vinegars for pickling. You can choose either white or apple cider vinegar. The biggest reason that I recommend commercial vinegars for beginners is because they are guaranteed to have 5% acidity, which is essential to the pickling process. Yes, you will probably be making homemade vinegar at some point, but the problem is that it's probably going to be less acidic than commercial brands.

Another important tip is to always label your pickle jars so that you know what's inside. Sometimes you won't be able to tell just by looking at it since pickling tends to change the aesthetics of the produce. Dating each jar is also important so that you know which ones to pull from the shelf.

It's pretty easy to get started with pickling so there's no reason why you can't try your hand at it. Pickling is a terrific way to gauge whether or not the homesteading life is for you.

Finally, be sure that you store your pickles in a cool place that is not in direct sunlight. Once you break the seal, you have to store them in the refrigerator. Also, if a jar leaks during storage, then it's compromised and should be thrown away.

Canning For Beginners

Canning is one of the fundamentals of homesteading since it gives you a way to store a large amount of produce over a long period of time. So this is definitely an activity I recommend trying right away so that you can start learning this essential task now.

With that said, you'll need to invest in a pressure canner in order to can foods that are low in acidity. Even if you plan to can recipes that contain both high and low acidity foods, you will still need a pressure canner. The reason is that water bath canners are not hot enough to kill bacteria of low acid foods.

In short, if you aren't pickling the food, and it's not considered a high acid food, then you will need a pressure canner in order to ensure all bacteria is eliminated.

Pressure canners are built with a locking lid and a gauge that regulates the steam pressure in the canner. Steam is allowed to build in the container, which reaches

240 degrees. This is a high enough temperature to destroy bacteria spores that are present in low acidic foods.

Water Bath Canning Versus Pressure Canning

Water bath canning can reach as high as 212 degrees. While this temperature works perfectly for preserving high acidic foods, it doesn't kill botulism spores that are formed in low acidic foods. Botulism is a dangerous and deadly pathogen that is found in canned foods.

That's where pressure canning comes into play. Pressure canning reaches a much higher temperature that destroys spores that cause botulism. However, this process requires specialized equipment. That's why so many people choose water bath canning.

Water Bath Canning Process

You'll need a large pot that's deep enough to submerge a jar so that the lid is at least one inch under the water. A stockpot or a lobster pot work if you don't have a water bath canner. It's also important that you use a rack so that the base of the jar doesn't touch the bottom of the pot and keep the jars separated. If they are allowed to rattle together, they might break or form fractures that will cause them to spoil.

Add the water to the pot and then bring the water to a boil. Temperatures should be 140 degrees for raw-packing and 180 degrees for hot packing.

While the water heats up, start prepping the jars. Inspect the rims for damage. If one is chipped or has any damage, don't use it. You also cannot reuse lids from previous canning, although it's okay to reuse the rings. Once you have verified that the lids are okay, wash the jars in hot water and then quickly dry them. You need to heat up the glass before it goes into the boiling water to keep them from rapid temperature changes.

Now fill the jars with your recipe. Every recipe has specific instruction about how much empty space to leave at the top of the jar, called "head space." Use a stirring stick to mix and tamp down the product once it's in the jar. This removes air bubbles that might have been trapped when you filled the jar.

Clean the rim of the jar with a wet paper towel or damp cloth before adding the lid. You want them to be finger tight so that air is allowed to escape them during the canning process.

Load the cans onto a rack and lower it into the water. Be very careful with them. Make sure at least a half-inch of space is left between jars to prevent them from banging together and breaking.

Crank up the heat to bring the water to a boil and then put a lid on the pot. You will boil the jars according to the recipe. You want the water to boil at a full, yet steady rate. If the water boils violently, then turn down the heat a bit.

Once the allotted time has elapsed, turn off the heat and give the jars five to ten minutes to settle as the water temperature lowers. Never suddenly remove them from the water, this can also cause breakage.

After the jars have settled, remove them from the water. Make sure they remain upright and that you do not let them bang against other jars. Place the jars on a countertop coated with a towel or a baking rack to cool. They need to rest here for at least 12 hours.

Finally, inspect the cooled jars to make sure they sealed correctly. You can do this by pressing down on the lid. They should be solid. If they wiggle, then it means that the jar did not seal correctly. Remove rings and test the lid again to see if it stays solid.

Pressure Canning Process

I recommend you start by wiping down the pressure canner to remove any dust that might have accumulated during storage. This includes the exterior, interior, and rack.

Once the pressure canner has been wiped down, add water according to the manufacturer's instructions. Now you're ready to turn on the heat.

Just like with water bath canning, you need to clean each jar before filling it with the recipe. You also want the jars to be hot if using a hot pack recipe before placing them in the pressure canner. Cold jars will break when rapidly exposed to hot temperatures so place cold packed jars into the canner before it comes to a boil.

Just like in water bath canning, stir and tamp down the produce in order to remove all air bubbles and then screw the lid into place. Put each jar in the basket provided with your canner and slowly lower them into the machine, leaving about a half-inch of space between each one.

Seal the pressure canner shut and follow the manufacturer's instructions for venting. Then you just wait on the machine to get the pressure to the appropriate level. This is found in the recipe. Start the timer.

Pay attention to the canner and raise the heat if the pressure falls below the desired amount. Do the opposite if the pressure gets too high.

Once the processing is finished, shut down the heat and allow everything to cool down. Give it at least an hour before doing anything. Do not open the canner before the pressure indicator shows that all the pressure has been released. Doing so puts you at serious risk for a burn injury.

If you're done canning for the day, you can just leave the jars where they are. But if you need to remove them, use the same setup as earlier. Place the jars on a countertop lined with a towel. Be sure to keep your face away from the steam.

Let the jars sit for 24 hours and then check to ensure each lid has sealed properly. It will be secure. If the lid pops when pressed on, then the seal did not activate.

For more details on water bath and pressure canning, check out my book "Homestead Canning" available in December 2023. For additional details visit my website https://www.TheGreenHomesteader.com.

Part 4

Start a Successful Homestead

Chapter 11

Providing for Your Family

In software development, one hour of research saves you 10 hours of development work. With homestead development, one hour might save you twice that and save you thousands of dollars in expensive mistakes! Research is a concept that's lost on a lot of people once they step out of school. But it's an important tool that should be used with any new venture.

So, it's important that you develop a plan to build a successful homestead. Let's start by looking at the three most critical areas to research before diving headfirst into this venture.

Start by researching different locations before you even think about buying a property.

- Are there neighbors?
- Would any local laws impact a homestead?
- What is the climate like in the area?

- Are the roads navigable in the winter?
- How long does each growing season last?

There are more questions that need to be answered but these five are a great place to start.

That brings us to researching the types of crops you want to grow. How well would these vegetables grow in the climate where you want to live? If not, what type and size of greenhouse will you need?

You should also compare growing seasons of the area to the crops you want to grow. Longer growing seasons will lead to more produce without the cost of a spendy greenhouse.

Finally, research the requirements for any livestock you plan to raise on your homestead. Find out how much land you will need, how much it costs to feed them, and the tools you will need to preserve their products.

With that being said, there is a point where you can get stuck in research mode. The key is to learn enough to get started but at some point, you just have to get your hands dirty and follow through with your plan. Don't skip research and planning but don't let yourself get consumed by them either. Analysis Paralysis is a real thing that has prevented many a would-be homesteader from realizing their dreams.

This chapter will show you how to create a great homesteading plan. And then how to put that plan into action. Some people literally spend their whole lives planning and never actually do anything. In short, they literally plan themselves to death. Yes, you will make mistakes. Everyone does, and there's no way to completely avoid mistakes and setbacks. The goal is to mitigate risk, not completely eliminate it.

Calculating Your Family's Needs

By this point, you already have a basic plan to move forward so it's time to focus it into more measurable steps. The ultimate goal of homesteading is to become self-sufficient, so you are able to meet the needs of your family. Therefore, it makes sense to determine exactly what those needs are.

Think of it like creating a budget. Production of your homestead is your income while your family's needs are the expenses. In order to be self-sufficient, your production must meet or exceed your needs.

How Many Vegetables Does your Family Need?

Knowing how much land you need for gardening is the easiest place to start. There really isn't a perfect answer here since everyone has specific needs. The basic rule of thumb is to plan for 200 square feet per person.

The problem is that since plants vary so drastically in size, 200 square feet might not be enough with certain types of vegetables. That's why I have created a handy gardening size chart along with a description

There are also other considerations to keep in mind. The size of your family is the most obvious. However, always plan for more because you're sure to have people over for dinner throughout the year. Those big dinners count! For example, if Sunday family dinners are a normal routine, then you need to account for food being eaten during those dinners. Generally, planning for 10% to 20% more than your family's needs is good practice.

I use and recommend the Square Foot ® gardening method and suggest you do also when planning your homestead garden. Raised bed gardens make sense for a couple of different reasons.

Firstly, and most importantly, it's easier to maintain. Because you are beginning with either new soil you have created using peat moss, vermiculite, and compost or raised bed gardening mix, you will be starting with a clean slate in regard to weeds and soil texture which means you'll require less digging, feeding, weeding, and watering.

Secondly, organizing and planning your garden is much simpler, because it is really easy to calculate how much of each vegetable or herb you can grow in a square foot.

It is also allowing you to easily create vertical gardening spaces to optimize your planting area so you can grow more produce in less than half [viii] the space of a traditional garden. So, to put it into perspective, you will need 200 sf per person in a traditional garden (about the size of two small bedrooms) or 48 sf raised bed (about ½ the size of one small bedroom). But regardless of which style of garden you choose, you can use the following charts to help determine how much produce to grow for each person in your family. Note that these charts represent the standard growing season with succession plantings for fresh produce. If you choose not to preserve vegetables and don't use green houses or cold frames to extend the growing season, you will only have enough fresh produce to last the growing cycle.

Your first step is to determine what types of vegetables your family likes to eat and how much of each type they eat during the year. If you are someone who plans your family's meals in advance, you will have a head start. You can begin by looking back at your meal plans for the past year to get an idea of how much of each vegetable you planned into your diet and reference the chart below to determine how many plants you need to grow the amount necessary to feed your family. This annual plan will give you your baseline and also identify how much extra you purchased for entertaining friends and family.

If you aren't an avid meal planner, don't despair, you can get similar information by looking at the past year's grocery receipts, or if you don't have them, by starting to save grocery receipts and adding up the amounts of produce purchased. If you do this for at least three months, you can then multiply the number by four to get a reasonable estimate to start planning for the next year's harvest. And don't forget to add canned foods. You can preserve almost anything you can grow and many of the things you can cook, so if you are buying canned tomatoes, spaghetti sauce, or chili, you can add in calculations for additional produce so you can preserve it for later. But remember… if you are new to gardening, having more produce than you can eat may be overwhelming if you don't already know how to can, pickle, or otherwise preserve your abundance, so start small and work your way up.

To get started, figure out the total number of pounds, gallons, bushels, etc. of each crop you will grow to meet your family's needs based on your annual meal plan. Next you will divide the per square foot yield to determine how many square feet of plantings will be necessary to produce the quantity you identified. Finally, you should start with the most common vegetables and identify early, mid, and late season varieties for as many of the vegetables as possible to ensure you have the longest harvest season.

For example, beans are a common vegetable and easy to grow. You can harvest approximately 1.5 lbs. per square foot if raised bed gardening. This assumes nine plants per square foot. If you are row gardening, you would plant approximately three linear feet. Note that all the calculations are based on the minimum spacing requirements for each plant type (These can be found on the seed package if you are starting from seed). Again, beans must be planted at least 4" apart which means you can plant nine plants per square foot, or a single row 3 feet long. The benefits for raised bed gardening become obvious quite quickly when calculating not only the space requirements, but also the maintenance requirements in a more compact garden.

The chart below shows estimated yields for commonly grown vegetables for both Square Foot ® gardening and row gardening.[ix] To determine planting quantities, multiply the number of people in the household by the desired harvest per person fresh and stored. Note that children, depending upon age, can be estimated at ¼ to ¾ the desired amount. The area necessary to produce the desired yield can be estimated by calculating the total quantity and dividing by the yield per square foot or linear ft.

If a household member does not like the vegetable, don't include it in the calculations. You can visit my website for a downloadable excel version of the garden area and planting quantity calculations.

Calculating Garden Space

The following table provides an example of the calculations workbook you'll find on my website https://www.TheGreenHomesteader.com. If you use this table, you will be able to estimate the amount of area necessary to grow all your produce. There is one important concept that will be explained in greater detail in the workbook relating to succession planting. If you are not familiar with the concept, it's the idea that you won't plant all the food at the same time. While some things take a long time to grow, like pumpkins, which you only harvest once, other things which have a short growing cycle, like lettuce, should be planted in smaller batches 7 to 21 days apart, hence the term succession planting. Succession planting allows you to have something ready for harvest at all times, rather than having 40 heads of lettuce becoming ready at the same time. It also gives you the same yearly harvest and uses less space. This is perfect for optimizing limited space and ensures that soil has roots in it all through growing season.

How Much Do I Grow Per Person?

As discussed earlier, the amount to grow per person will vary, but the following table will give you some idea of how much you can expect to harvest under perfect conditions. Remember we discussed adding in a few more plants to account for loss due to weather and pests, as well as for feeding the family when they drop by for dinner.

Homesteading for Beginners: A Budget-Friendly Path to Self-Reliance

Vegetable	Desired Harvest in Lbs Per Person - Fresh	Desired Harvest in Lbs Per Person- Store or Preserve	Harvest in Lbs Per Square Foot -SF Gardening Method	Harvest in Lbs Per Linear Foot-Row Gardening
Potatoes	25	75	16	1.5
Corn*	25 ears	50 ears	4 - 8 ears	1 -2 ear
Carrots	10	10	2	1.2
Tomatoes*	24	20	1.5	1.5
Zucchini	10	5	6	2.5
Squash	6	3	5	2.5
Pumpkin	10	8	7.5	4
Broccoli	8	2	0.75	0.5
Cauliflower	9	12	2	1
Peppers	3	3.5	3	1
Celery	4	10	4	4
Sweet Potatoes	3	3.5	1.5	0.5
Beans	15	1.3	1.5	1
Peas	4.5	7.5	1	0.75
Lettuce*	6	N/A	4	0.5
Chard	1	2.5	1	1
Kale	1	2.5	1	1
Onions	8	20	6	1.25
Garlic	1	10	2	1.25
Eggplant	4	10	2	2
Asparagus	1.5	5	1	0.25
Spinach	3	5	2	0.5
Brussel Sprouts	6	2	1.25	0.3
Melons*	12	5	7	3

Table 1: How Much to Grow Per Person

* These amounts are estimated based on information from various agricultural websites and some plants may produce more or less depending upon the variety and growing conditions.

Efficient Use of Gardening Space

You can get the most from land space by rotating multiple plants throughout the year. This is known as succession planting, which we discussed briefly in the previous section.

Another thing to consider is crop rotation. Crop rotation prevents using up all the natural resources in the soil.

Scientists at the Rodale Institute[x] warn against planting the same crop in the same place every year. Not only does it draw the same nutrients from the soil, but it also encourages pests and diseases since they know where to find their preferred food source. Crop rotation will help return nutrients to the soil since some plants actually increase certain nutrients.

For Example:

- Grow peas first. Peas add nitrogen to the soil.
- Once the peas are harvested, grow green beans in the same soil. Green beans thrive from the added nitrogen.
- Harvest green beans and plant peas again.

You can rotate through these two crops or find other crops with the same properties and increase the rotation to include three or even four different crops. It also saves on fertilizer since you are replenishing nutrients into the soil naturally.

How Much Meat Will Your Family Consume?

I don't recommend raising a lot of animals during your first year of homesteading. It would likely be too overwhelming. Instead, it's best to stay focused on learning to grow vegetables first, even if you don't intend to raised bed garden. Take the first year to gain some experience and confidence with succession planting and to learn your unique property's planting zones. You may want to invest in a small chicken coop, but that's as far as I would go if you don't already have experience with animals.

With that said, it's okay to go ahead and plan for the day when you decide to take on animals. Setting goals helps keep you focused even if intend to wait a year or two before putting the plan into action.

Here's a chart that shows the average meat consumption in the US based on data from 2019.

Meat	Consumption (lbs.) Family Size 1/2/3/4	Pounds of Meat Produced by Each Animal After Processing
Beef	58/116/174/232	460 Lbs.
Pork	52/104/156/208	104 Lbs.
Chicken	95/190/285/380	3.5 to 5 Lbs.
Turkey	16/32/48/64	16 to 22 Lbs.

Table 2: Meat Consumption in the US

Planning for animals gets tricky because you won't want to raise every different type without prior experience. You'll likely choose to focus on only one or two at most. Plus, you will also need to consider dairy animals if that's one of your goals. We'll look at that more in a moment.

My point is that you need to plan all of it as a whole and figure out how to meet your needs. For instance, if you have a family of four, then one cow would give you twice the amount of beef necessary to be self-sufficient. So, you could sell the excess beef and use that money to buy fresh pork from another farmer.

If you are raising dairy, then you will be breeding cows so you might not even need to raise goats or pigs since you would have so much excess beef that you could just sell it or barter it for pork.

These are just some examples of why it's so important to plan your homestead thoroughly. There's really no need to raise every single type of animal. Heck, just one dairy cow and a chick coop for eggs will produce plenty of meat to meet most family's needs.

Chapter 12

Set Your Finalized Goals

Homesteading goals are paramount during your first year. They will likely make or break your success. Most new ventures succeed or fail based on the first year so it's absolutely essential that you get this right. There's absolutely no way you can take on this much responsibility without having specific, measurable goals to keep you on track. As previously mentioned, you can visit my website for a free copy of my budget planner and goal-setting workbook. This will help you set SMART goals.

SMART goals are:

> S: Specific
> M: Measurable
> A: Achievable
> R: Relevant
> T: Time-bound

Setting goals doesn't necessarily mean that you won't change things up as you go. But you need a roadmap of some kind to keep you working in the right direction. I can tell you from experience that if you don't plan appropriately, then you risk having to redo a lot of the things you do during the first year. We had to replace a whole fence because we rushed it. Planning would have saved us a lot of time and expense, not to mention spared us the headache!

By this point in the book, I imagine you have laid out several goals and have a good idea of the direction you want to go. So now it's time to finalize all of those goals. It's important to put them in writing, draw up important dates on the calendar, and make it all official. Doing so will help motivate you and keep you accountable.

Start this process by documenting your main reason for homesteading. We discussed this in a previous chapter so it's time to finalize this reason and give it a tangible format. Write this down somewhere so you can look at it every day. It will be your main motivation. I cannot overemphasize how important motivation is during your first year on the homestead. There are so many activities going on, that it's easy to get distracted. These distractions cause us to switch focus from our long-term goals and plans to tasks that seem like quick wins. Some of these seemingly quick wins have consequences you hadn't considered and will likely end up in rework.

Year One Expectations

Unless you come into a lot of money, you will probably have to juggle modern living with homesteading during the initial phases. That means the majority of your tasks will be carried out on weekends and in the evening after work. Be absolutely sure that your goals take this into account. Your time is limited so you can only do so much. It's far more important to do each task the right way rather than just throwing stuff together and having to redo it later.

Since you will be juggling a lot of different jobs at once, you must stay organized. You don't want to wait until you get home from work to decide what tasks you'll be doing. Plan this stuff ahead of time so you can just follow a list.

Invest in a planner to keep track of everything you need to do. There is a printable page included in the Budget Planner and Goal-Setting workbook on my website to get you started. https://www.TheGreenHomesteader.com.

Your calendar will not only list your important goals, but your planner tells you the daily steps you must take in order to achieve those goals. Here's an easy-to-follow process:

1. First, choose a day each week to designate as your planning day. On that day, choose one task for your focus. This should be something that leads to the growth of your homestead. By now you should have identified at least one goal and all the tasks that are associated with it, as well as the estimated expenses, and captured that information in the planner.
2. Next, fill in your planner with chores that must be completed. These are generally not part of your focus. They are everyday homesteading activities like watering the garden, cleaning the chicken coop, or gathering eggs.
3. Finally, fill in remaining time on your planner with tasks that work toward your focus.

It's important to pace yourself appropriately. You can't do everything at once and homesteading can be so overwhelming that it's easy to get burnt out if you dive in headfirst. Remember, it's okay to plan a day off every week to rest and recover. If you try to take on too much at once, you will probably get burnt out and give up.

Another consideration is that you will identify more chores as your homestead grows. Chores will eat away at your time, and you'll eventually reach the peak of what's possible. This is why having your end goal defined is such an important step. Only grow your homestead in ways that work toward that specific end goal.

Gardening

Gardening is likely the first major undertaking for new homesteaders. It is the foundation of sustainable living, so it makes sense to approach this first. I can tell you from experience that having a gardening plan will make your life a million times easier! Let's start with the basics.

The first thing you'll need is a sun map. Keep in mind that this isn't required if you are gardening in a clear area. On the other hand, if there are any obstructions around, then you need to map out the area to find the best place for your garden. In layman's terms, a sun map is simply an estimate of how much sunlight specific areas on your property receives on a daily basis.

Plants need at least six hours of sunlight, sometimes more depending on the exact crop being grown. It's best to try to find a gardening space that gets 8 to 10 hours of sunlight every day.

Identify your Growing Zone

Learning about growing zones is the most important piece of information you will ever learn about homesteading. The concept is actually simple. Geographic locations are great for developing certain types of plants. The crop can survive even in the lowest temperatures of that area. It's essential that you grow plants that are recommended for specific geographical locations.

The USDA calls this the hardiness zone and they have created a map of the United States that will show you the best plants to grow in each zone within the country. In short, the USDA categorizes using a main category and subcategory. Everything is based on annual minimum winter temperatures

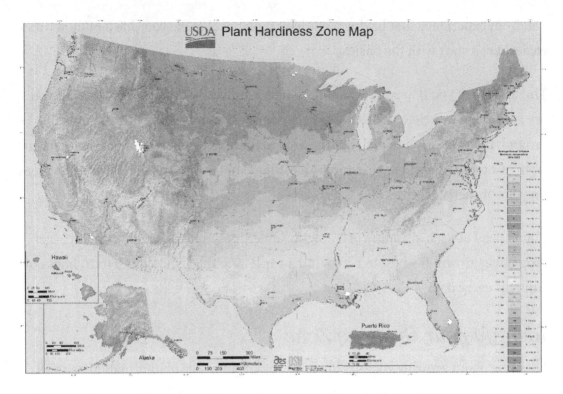

Figure 1: US Hardiness Zone Map

A color coded and more detailed breakdown for the US can be found at https://pdi.scinet.usda.gov/phzm/md/All_states_halfzones_poster_300dpi.jpg.

The detailed image breaks down the numbered categories into numbered and lettered categories. The numbered category separates regions by 10 degrees while the lettered category further breaks down regions into 5-degree segments.

The USDA website also provides an interactive map that will allow you to zoom to your location.
https://planthardiness.ars.usda.gov/

Each country will have an official website to provide detailed hardiness information, but

Figure 5: Hardiness Scale

for a quick reference you can use the following map. Please visit the website for a full color image.

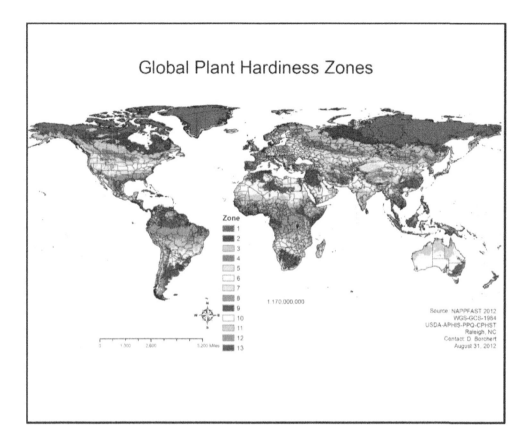

Figure 3: Global Hardiness Zones - This work is in the public domain in the United States because it is a work prepared by an officer or employee of the United States Government as part of that person's official duties under the terms of Title 17, Chapter 1, Sec

The concept of the map is that the growing zone shows you how cold the winter months can be in your specific location. Plants are recommended based on that metric. In short, you just identify your location on the map, look at your category, and then find recommended plants. Seed packets will often include the safe planting dates by zone. Http://www.PlantMaps.com provides an interactive hardiness zone map.

Take Note of Frost Dates

Growing zones also reveal the first and last frost days of the year so you need to take note of this since it helps you better plan your garden. You can determine the optimal growing season by counting the days between the last frost day (occurs in Spring) and the first frost day (occurs Fall or Winter). Lower numbered zones will have shorter growing seasons.

You can use this information to create a detailed garden plan. You'll find that certain plants thrive in warm weather while others are just fine in cooler temperatures which will help you identify not only what to plant and when to plant it, but plants that need special precautions for either summer heat or winter cold. For instance, carrots, broccoli, and lettuce are all highly resilient to cold weather so you want to grow them early and late in your planting season. On that same note, cold weather plants don't tend to do well in the hot summer months.

Tomatoes, peppers, and potatoes on the other hand are all warm season plants that thrive in hot temperatures so they should be grown right in the middle of your growing season.

Here's a handy chart that includes the average frost dates by zone.

PLANTING ZONES

ZONE	AVERAGE LAST FROST DATE	AVERAGE FIRST FROST DATE
Zone 1	May 22-June 4	August 25-31
Zone 2	May 15-22	September 1-8
Zone 3	May 1-6	September 8-15
Zone 4	April 24-May 12	September 21-October 7
Zone 5	April 7-30	October 13-21
Zone 6	April 1-12	October 17-31
Zone 7	March 22-April 3	October 20-November 15
Zone 8	March 13-28	November 7-28
Zone 9	February 6-28	November 25-December 13
Zone 10	Usually No Frost	Usually No Frost
Zone 11	Usually No Frost	Usually No Frost
Zone 12	Usually No Frost	Usually No Frost
Zone 13	Usually No Frost	Usually No Frost

Figure 7: Planting Zone Average Frost Dates

The final step is to lay out your garden. Determine what seeds to plant and when you will start them. Estimate the harvest times for succession planting and try to rotate the plants so that the soil stays healthy.

Determine What Structures You Need to Build

Fencing and overall construction in general is a lengthy process. This can't be done overnight so it's important that you lay this out in small, manageable steps. There are a number of limiting factors like budget, time, and materials that will completely bottleneck this process if not planned properly.

First, make sure you take the time to get it right. Again, you don't want to have to rebuild a fence two years down the line because you rushed. This is expensive and stressful. Especially when the neighbors are calling because your goat just ravaged their garden.

So, if you plan on raising livestock, then proper fencing is a requirement. Even if you are planning to focus on gardening during your first year, you can go ahead and start building areas for potential livestock that will be added in the future. I highly recommend that you plan this out now and start building the appropriate security. This gives you plenty of time to get it right since you won't have to rush.

Here are a few types of fencing and their best uses:

- **Hardware Cloth Fencing:** Perfect for chicken coops because it's much more reliable than chicken wire. Cloth fencing offers superior protection from predators. Note that it's not made out of cloth, it gets its name from the way the fence is woven.
- **Pasture Paddock:** Designed for larger animals like cows or other grazers. This is a permanent fence area that covers an entire pasture. It's separated into sections so you can move cattle from one section of the pasture to the other. This can be created using many fencing materials and is intended to be strong enough to keep even the largest animal in its proper place.
- **Portable Electric Fencing:** This is used for chickens, goats, sheep, and other small animals. The advantage is that portable electric fencing comes in a long roll so it's not only easy to install, but also easy to move. This is great if you are free ranging chickens in an area with a lot of predators. I have three rolls of it on my farm.

Fences are only one step though. If you ever plan to build a sustainable homestead, then you'll need a few essential structures. A woodshed is a given if you plan to use wood heating. Storing wood outdoors allows mold and rot to set into it, making it less efficient. A small woodshed doesn't take a lot to build, and it will make a world of difference. There are also simple to create racks that can be covered with tarps if that is your preference.

Of course, a chicken coop is another must for homesteaders since chickens provide a lot of benefits for relatively minimal effort. Just stay away from chicken wire and temporary coops. Give yourself time to build a proper chicken coop using cloth fencing and a sturdy roof. Secure it against predators so that you have one less worry.

As your homestead grows, you will find yourself with a lot of equipment so you will eventually need somewhere to store it, so don't forget to plan out space for an equipment shed. Not only will it give you a single place to store all your tools and equipment, but it will also protect them from the weather so they will last longer.

Creating a Layout of Your Homestead

One of the biggest misconceptions is the belief that self-sufficiency requires a lot of land. The fact is that it's possible to create a self-sufficient homestead on a small piece of land. You just have to lay it out efficiently. That's where planning comes into play. Here are some important considerations to keep in mind before you start laying out your homestead.

First of all, agriculture is not sustainable over the long-term without animals. Plant-only fertilizer is not going to provide the soil with adequate nutrients. Plants feed on the nutrients in soil so it is slowly depleted. While some of it can be recovered through plant-based fertilizers, it won't be enough to sustain the garden.

On the other hand, combining animal-based fertilizers, like composted chicken droppings, adds the proper nutrients to the soil so it not only becomes sustainable, but it also gains regenerative properties over time. In short, you need both plants and animals to build a sustainable lifestyle.

Rabbits are a great addition since they have low upkeep, breed rapidly, and their manure is the only manure that doesn't need to be composted before applying it to the garden.

Sheep and goat pellets are also both great choices for fertilizer since their manure contains a lot of nitrogen. And sheep pellets are not only high in nitrogen, but also potassium. Just remember they need to be composted with their bedding before being applied to the garden.

Another important consideration is whether or not you want to raise pigs. Smaller homesteads are not a good choice for raising pigs since they will destroy land and they smell horrid. You may want to consider bartering for pork if it's a meat you absolutely must have for your family, and you don't have a lot of space.

Grain is a poor choice for small farms since it takes a lot of space for little payout. If you own a smaller property, then you have to be efficient. Grain is not exactly known for its efficiency.

If you choose to raise dairy, then you will be limited even further on a smaller property. Cows are difficult to fit into a smaller homestead. It's possible, but not the most efficient approach. Goats are a much better choice for dairy on a small homestead.

Finally, try keeping animals separated as much as possible. This limits the transfer of disease and keeps the animals from becoming temperamental.

Okay! Now it's time to draw the homestead diagram and lay out what you've planned in your head. Don't worry about drawing everything perfectly. Remember that this is a reference and not something you'll show at an art exhibit! Just keep everything as close to scale as possible. Grid paper is an excellent choice for keeping everything in scale.

1. Start by adding your home to the diagram. Give enough space around the home for a small yard.
2. Add strawberries, herbs, and other decorative plants strategically around your home. This gives your home aesthetic appeal while also growing something you'll use.
3. Lay out your garden area based on your sun chart. Choose the location that gets the most sunlight. The best bet is to assign 25% of your homestead land to gardening unless you are using raised beds, in which case you can plan for

less. Just use the charts and information in the previous chapter to help you determine how big that space should be.
4. Add in a chicken coop. The size will depend on the needs of your family as determined in the previous chapters of the book.
5. Lay out the locations of your structures like a wood storing shed, equipment storage, and other necessities. Try to place them all together, where possible, so they share walls since it saves money and space.
6. Plan some areas for animals like goats, sheep, or rabbits. These will need to be fenced in so draw out the fence that will surround the area.

These are just the basics so you will probably have room left on the diagram to add in other stuff. This is your choice. If you want to raise bees, then add in a beehive. If you want to plant some cherry trees, then do so. Just be sure you use every inch of your property for something useful. It's okay to leave them blank for now and fill in these spaces later.

Once your property has been diagramed, you will find that it's much easier to keep on track. But now comes the hard part – execution of the plan.

Chapter 13

Create a Plan of Execution

Congratulations! You've finally made it to the execution stage so now it's time to start the real work. One of the most frustrating things when starting out is that there seem to be a million things to do, and you only have a limited amount of time. So, take a deep breath and wipe all of that worry from your mind. You have all of your long-term goals laid out and have even drawn a diagram of your future homestead. There's no need to let any expectations crush you. You know how your homestead will look several years from now so for now just focus on short-term goals.

The first rule is that you have to prioritize your tasks since time and money will both limit your progress. So before filling out your planner for week one, it's important to learn how to prioritize. Once you have begun creating the planned spaces you have to know where to focus your energy.

Always Prioritize People First

Always put the health of yourself and your family above all else when planning your daily tasks. Don't overwork yourself or do anything that compromises your safety.

The tasks will still be there tomorrow, but people are priceless. If you start pushing people just because you need to get things done, then you risk breaking those people – including yourself.

After all, the whole idea of building a self-sufficient lifestyle is to escape the stress of modern living. You're just defeating the purpose if you push yourself or your family to the breaking point. It's not worth it.

Taking regular breaks and addressing people problems should always come first.

Animals are Second

Once you have added animals to the homestead, their priority comes after people but should be prioritized over other homesteading tasks. All of your farm animals are dependent on you for everything so issues with them must be resolved first. If predators are getting into their pens, then it must be fixed. If they are sick, then their health must be a priority.

Aside from being humane, animals are harder and more expensive to replace than crops.

In the early stages of your homestead, you probably won't have many animals, so emergencies won't be an issue. But you should still prioritize all housing in preparation of adding them at a later date. Remember, your garden is not sustainable without having animals on your homestead unless you have another reliable source for chemical free compost.

Equipment and Tools Come Before Plants

The bottom line is that plants are much easier to replace than equipment so always keep the maintenance of your equipment as a higher priority. Tools require love and care in order to remain functional. It's much more affordable to go out and buy produce to replace a garden than it would be to buy a new tractor!

Be sure that you add machine maintenance to your schedule and leave yourself adequate time to put away all of the tools you use every day. Build a storage shed as quickly as possible so that your tools and equipment have a home. This should be a high priority during your first year.

Land Management

As we know, the health of your garden depends on how well you manage the land. Make sure you prioritize building a compost pile and gathering manure so that you can fertilize garden soil between harvests. This is essential to building a sustainable homestead.

Also, roads should be properly maintained, and animals should not be allowed to overgraze their pastures. If you effectively manage land, then the only problems that will pop up are emergencies that have obvious priorities.

In short, land management and gardening are tied in terms of priority so work them into your schedule as needed.

Gardening

As previously discussed, gardening is the foundation to creating a self-sufficient lifestyle so you might be surprised that it's at the bottom of our list of priorities. Well as I said bluntly in an earlier section, the garden is the easiest to replace. You can just buy produce from other farmers if the worst were to happen. Everything else on your homestead is much more difficult to replace.

I'm not encouraging you to ignore your garden. It is essential to the sufficiency of your homestead. But so are the people, animals, and equipment. Hopefully, you never have to decide between them. In most scenarios, there's enough time to deal with emergencies and still find time to care for your garden.

Identify Tasks and Make a To-Do List

Now, it's time to list all of the tasks that are required in order to achieve your overall homesteading goals. Just keep in mind that if an emergency pops up, then you will need to handle it immediately.

Tasks are broken down using the following criteria:

- Tasks that **NEED** to be done.
- Tasks you **WANT** to do.
- What **RESOURCES** are required to complete the task?
- What kind of **RETURN** will you get when completing this task?

The best way to approach this is to write down every task you need to achieve in order to meet your homesteading goals. I recommend that you use a spreadsheet to make this easier.

Separate these items into needs and wants. Items that need to be completed are a higher priority. For instance, building a chicken coop would be a need since it's required to start producing your own eggs. Adding a flower garden would classify as a want rather than a need unless you are planning to sell flowers at the local farmer's market as another source of income.

Next, add four columns to the spreadsheet and title them as **Time**, **Cost**, **Resources** and **Return**. Fill in that information for each item on the list.

- **Time:** An estimated time to complete the task.
- **Cost:** An estimated cost to complete the task.
- **Resources:** List everything you need to complete the task. This includes materials, tools, and skillset.
- **Return:** What will you get once the task is completed? For example, the return on a chicken coop would be a steady flow of eggs.

You'll find that having everything neatly organized makes decisions so much easier. You know what resources you have at your disposal, what skills you have, and what you can afford. So now it's just a matter of setting priorities.

Go through this list and order everything based on their level of importance. Using the goal of "build a chicken coop" as an example again, we can assume that would be a high priority since it's an affordable goal that produces eggs.

Adding fencing would be another high priority item since it protects everything within the homestead. How you list these items greatly depends on your family's preferences and the goals you have set for your homestead.

Weekly Planning Made Simple

At this point, you'll be observing your homestead, laying out a weekly plan, and then taking action. Set aside a day to plan out a whole week at a time. List all of the chores that are required to operate your homestead. Once that's done, you will be filling in the blanks with tasks from your list. That list will guide you to your long-term homesteading goals.

I learned quickly that I had to be open to learning and adapting to new situations. Unexpected things happen quite often on a homestead, so you have to become a master of observation. Be prepared to lose time addressing emergencies. Trust me, they do happen and that's okay. Just deal with them and move back to your list.

Get into the habit of using your planner and scheduling your time efficiently. Planning makes your whole journey so much easier.

Final Thoughts

Let's end this book by addressing something that none of us like talking about but we all know will happen. Setbacks are inevitable. We all find ourselves in slumps when it seems the whole world is against us. Homesteading is tough so these slumps are especially draining. It's important that you work past them.

The biggest problem is that slumps can come from anywhere. They don't necessarily emerge from the homestead itself. A lot of challenges you'll face form away from the homestead, forcing you to continue juggling your homesteading responsibilities with these challenges. During these times, your new simple lifestyle might seem more complicated than ever!

First and foremost, just remember that you will face challenges in all walks of life. There's no way to escape them. Life is all about perseverance and adaptability. Whatever you do, don't become discouraged!

Homesteaders have a lot of grit and heart, so turn to those qualities to push through difficult times. Let your determination fuel you. Don't wait for the unfortunate circumstances to catch up with you. Start taking action as quickly as possible. You have a homesteading plan so keep following it. Trust your plan but also be willing to adapt it if necessary.

The best way to end this book is to remind you that when adversity strikes, never let it rip away your heart. You are a homesteader so I'm willing to bet that if you made it this far, then you're tough as nails. Start taking small steps to resolve the problem and keep at it. Eventually, you will conquer it.

About the Author

Elise Baker is the founder of The Green Homesteader, a website committed to providing quality content related to homesteading. She is an avid gardener who not only loves to hear about new tips and time saving techniques, but also loves to share her knowledge and skills with others so that they can reap the benefits of shared experience and have more time to spend with their families. To stay on top of trending topics in sustainable agriculture she follows such greats as Joel Salatin and William Horvath. Their books, websites, and training have added to the planning, design, and maintenance of her 16.5-acre homestead in Tennessee where she lives with her husband, son, four dogs, four cats, and 23 chickens.

Your Opinion Matters!

Thank you for reading this book. I hope it has helped you get one step closer to living the dream of a simpler life.

Every reader's opinion is important, so I have a request to make. I would be forever grateful if you could leave a review of this book. Reviews will help me learn from this experience and improve all books I publish in the future. Book reviews help create a better reading experience for everyone. Your thoughts and opinions will help readers like you get started on the road to self-reliance.

Thanks, and I look forward to seeing your reviews.

Oh… And don't forget your free bonus content. Scan the QR codes below for your Free Budget Planner and Goal Setting Workbook and the Free Planting Calculator if you haven't already done so!

Visit https://www.TheGreenHomesteader.com to get a link to your free downloadable content or scan the QR codes below.

Square Foot
Garden Calculator

Budget Planner &
SMART Goals Workbook

References

[i] https://wayback.archive-it.org/5774/20220413204627/https://www.healthypeople.gov/2020/leading-health-indicators/2020-lhi-topics/Nutrition-Physical-Activity-and-Obesity

[ii] https://www.thelancet.com/journals/lanplh/article/PIIS2542-5196(19)30215-3/fulltext

[iii] Donald R. Davis, PhD, FACN, Melvin D. Epp, PhD and Hugh D. Riordan, MD, "Changes in USDA Food Composition Data for 43 Garden Crops, 1950 to 1999," Journal of the American College of Nutrition, 2004.

[iv] https://www.fda.gov/vaccines-blood-biologics/consumers-biologics/asthma-hygiene-hypothesis#:~:text=According%20to%20the%20%E2%80%9Chygiene%20hypothesis,defense%20responses%20to%20infectious%20organisms

[v] https://www.irs.gov/pub/irs-pdf/p225.pdf

[vi] https://www.irs.gov/pub/irs-pdf/f1040sf.pdf

[vii] https://www.irs.gov/pub/irs-pdf/p225.pdf

[viii] (https://www.almanac.com/video/how-many-garden-to-feed-family)

[ix] Note that yields will vary by growing location, season, experience, pests, etc. I've provided estimates to get you started, but you will want to keep your own records, so you know what to expect based on the gardening style, soil type, and soil condition on your homestead.

[x] Visit https://rodaleinstitute.org/ for more information about organic and regenerative farming methods.

Made in United States
North Haven, CT
24 February 2024

49143459R00085